homeless mothers

Published with assistance from the Margaret S. Harding
Memorial Endowment honoring the first director
of the University of Minnesota Press.

homeless mothers

FACE TO FACE WITH WOMEN AND POVERTY

Deborah R. Connolly

University of Minnesota Press Minneapolis London

Published by the University of Minnesota Press
111 Third Avenue South, Suite 290
Minneapolis, MN 55401-2520
http://www.upress.umn.edu

Library of Congress Cataloging-in-Publication Data

Connolly, Deborah R., 1969–
    Homeless mothers : face to face with women and poverty / Deborah R.
Connolly.
        p.   cm.
    Includes bibliographical references and index.
    ISBN 0-8166-3281-2 (jkt. hard : alk. paper) — ISBN 0-8166-3282-0 (alk. paper)
    1. Homeless women—Oregon—Case studies.   2. Homeless families—
Oregon—Case studies.   3. Social services—Oregon—Case studies.   I. Title:
Face to face with women and poverty.   II. Title.
HV4506.O76 C66 2000
362.83′086′942—dc21   99-050683

Printed in the United States of America on acid-free paper

The University of Minnesota is an equal-opportunity educator and employer.

11 10 09 08 07 06 05 04 03 02 01 00   10 9 8 7 6 5 4 3 2 1

Contents

Acknowledgments

My interest in cultural analysis did not spring from nowhere. I have been fortunate to be surrounded by brilliant academics, caring and persistent friends, and an amazing and supportive family. While I cannot hold them responsible for this or any of my other endeavors, I do want to recognize the inspirational teachings that they have provided on so many registers and that have enabled me to engage this work.

As an undergraduate at the University of Massachusetts, Amherst, I received valuable attention from creative minds who introduced me to the academic world and nurtured me through various hesitancies and wayward visions. In particular I want to thank Charles Adams, Lee Edwards, Patricia Mangan, Sandra Morgen, and Jacqueline Urla for all their resourcefulness and direction.

As a doctoral student at the University of California, Santa Cruz, I was very fortunate to have a reflective, insightful, and supportive dissertation committee—Anna Lowenhaupt Tsing, Wendy Brown, and Susan Harding. I am grateful for all their advice, prodding, suggestions, and infectious enthusiasm. Their careful readings of my dissertation were indispensable. I have been inspired by their work, both written and in the classroom. I also want to thank Daniel Linger, who worked closely with me on this research and all the preliminary work that led up to it. His insight and interest were immensely valuable.

As I worked to transform my dissertation into a book, I benefited greatly from the engaged reading of Valerie Hartouni and the continued intellectual support of Wendy Brown and Anna Lowenhaupt Tsing. Amazingly, my undergraduate mentor became once again formative in my work, and I thank Sandra Morgen for her careful and productive reviews of this manuscript. And of course, I would not have been able to even begin this transformation without the faith and support of my editor at the University of Minnesota Press, Carrie Mullen.

This work would have been impossible were it not for the open dialogue shared by the staff and clients I worked with during my fieldwork in Portland. I want to acknowledge all the men, women, and children who took the time to tell their stories and offer their perspectives, and I only hope that this work in some ways begins to do justice to the insight and power they offered me.

Throughout these challenges I have been sustained by a dynamic group of friends who have seen me through this process in more ways than are imaginable. Many have offered their editorial ideas, some their homes and lives to share, and all their humor, patience, confidence, time, energy, and care. My thanks here cannot possibly do justice to all they have shared, but it will have to suffice for now. My deepest thanks to Jessica Basile, Amy Barg, Christian Dreyfus, Joanna Schwartz, Christine Selig, Galen Joseph, Michelle Rosenthal, Cori Ladd, Charlene Worley, Cimon Swanson, Valerie Ross, Lorraine Kenny, and Teresa Taylor.

I want to thank members of my family who have always been there for me in this study and in the millions of things that came before it, and who I have faith will be there in all those processes that follow (all I can really say is "Thank goodness for that"). My warmest love and thanks to Judith Connolly, Paula Richards, David Connolly, Jeanne Delaney, William Connolly, and Jane Bennett.

Finally, my immeasurable love, appreciation, and joy to James Youngblood, who has revitalized my life and painted my world with an infinite horizon of possibilities.

Key Figures

There are numerous people described throughout *Homeless Mothers*. To aid the reader I have compiled a list of key figures who are represented in the ethnography, using one or two indicators to help keep them straight. Since the book is organized around the mothers, I have set up the client list in family groups. All of the names are fictitious, although I have attempted to maintain the feel of the original name as much as possible—that is, if someone had an unusual and lyrical name, I tried to pick an equivalent one.

Clients

Kristy—Twenty-six-year-old white woman
Tim—Kristy's first husband, father of her two children
Joe—Kristy's current boyfriend
JR—Kristy's son
Sue Ellen—Kristy's daughter

Sally—Thirty-three-year-old white woman, mother of three boys between the ages of eight and twelve

Key Figures

Terry—Nineteen-year-old mixed-race woman (Dutch and Native American)
Carlos—Terry's first husband, father of her two children
Braley—Terry's son
Serene—Terry's daughter
Tommy—Terry's current boyfriend

Michelle—Twenty-year-old white woman
Tony—Michelle's boyfriend, father of her two children
Marissa—Michelle's daughter
Anthony Jr.—Michelle's newborn son

Hannah—Twenty-five-year-old white woman
Joe—Hannah's husband and father of her youngest two children
Bobby—Hannah's oldest son
Amber—Hannah's daughter (middle child)
Hannah's youngest son (unnamed)

Jane—Twenty-seven-year-old white woman
John—Jane's boyfriend and father of her second child
Angela—Jane's older daughter
Jane's younger daughter (unnamed)

Ruth—Thirty-year-old white woman
Ruth's husband (unnamed)
Tyler—Ruth's son
Lily—Ruth's daughter

Melanie—Thirty-six-year-old white woman
Jeff—Melanie's first husband and father of her first child (Duke)
Duke—Melanie's oldest son
Melanie's second husband and younger two children (unnamed)

Key Figures

Grace—Nineteen-year-old Latina woman
Matt—Grace's boyfriend
Kenyon—Matt and Grace's son
Carolyn—Matt's mother

Westside Community Center Staff

Margaret—Program director, white woman, midthirties
Miranda—Drug and alcohol specialist, white woman, late forties
Justin—Administrative assistant, white man, early sixties
Barry—Day shelter monitor/program assistant, Black man, midthirties
Jenny—Case manager, white woman, midtwenties
Sandy—Case manager/program supervisor, white woman, midfifties
Jared—Case manager, white man, midthirties
Jack—Housing coordinator, white man, midthirties

Introduction

Headlines

Mom on Trial in Fatal Crash for Not Using Tot's Seat Belt

Lesia Smith Pappas, 33, is accused of vehicular manslaughter in the death of two-year-old Alex Pappas. He died when Pappas lost control of her van while driving the other children to school in June 1995. She faces a possible maximum sentence of six years in prison.

Pappas is on trial, prosecutors say, because none of her children were wearing a seat belt when the van went out of control while going an estimated 65 mph.

"We're saying that she's a bad mother," said Deputy District Attorney Robert B. Fultz Jr. "She never cared about her kids enough to strap them in."

(San Jose Mercury News, July 21, 1996)

Officials Face Dilemma of Getting Tough without Hurting Children: Welfare Reform Efforts Trap Kids in the Middle

"The problem we're seeing with kids is not that their mama doesn't have enough money," Murray [a fellow at the American

Enterprise Institute] said. "You have women who are utterly incompetent at being mothers."

(*San Jose Mercury News*, March 14, 1994, 5A)

In Tests of Mice, a Gene Seems to Hold Clues to the Nature of Nurturing

Mutant mice that ignore their own infants, allowing them to die from neglect, provide new evidence that in mammals the very essence of mothering—the ability to nurture the young—has an important genetic component.

(*New York Times*, July 26, 1996, A7)

Consider the representation and production of motherhood in the above excerpts. How is motherhood framed, explained, and explored here? Who is doing the interpreting of motherhood and how? While lawyers, researchers, and scientists do not exhaust the list of those invested in particular cultural characterizations of motherhood, their contributions are significant to the growing idea that motherhood is something that needs intensive intervention to ensure its adequacy and alignment with cultural norms. Perhaps these excerpts also inadvertently expose the very *unnaturalness* of motherhood by revealing how much women who mother are culturally regulated, judged, and dissected, how their motherhood is a constant subject of interrogation in courtrooms, laboratories, and think tanks.

As contemporary culture becomes increasingly complex, technologized, and disciplinary, the image of a pristine motherhood lost becomes very appealing. Some anthropologists have participated in the construction of this nostalgia for a world lost, providing accounts of non-Western birthing practices in which women are seen to actualize their natural reproductive instincts in uncomplicated places such as "birthing huts," rather than the high-technology birthing arenas typical of U.S. culture today.

Such nostalgia imagines a simple world set in contrast to the turbulence of contemporary life. It also supports a backlash against feminist activism that has drawn women into work careers, public life, and higher education. Here, much of contemporary culture is seen to interfere with women's maternal functions rather than to civilize and enhance them. If women could reduce confusing career pursuits, curtail nonprocreative sexual desires, and transcend culturally induced selfish orientations, they might return to more nurturing practices of motherhood.

The contemporary model of the good mother emerges from this cultural climate. This model assumes as its implicit background a rather high level of income, a two-parent stable family, and significant control over one's own destiny. For many, the impossibility of attaining such conditions means that they are held accountable to standards impossible to meet. Would a good mother sleep with her children in a car parked on a city street in the middle of winter? Would a good mother send her child to school in shoes two sizes too large because that's all she could drum up? Would a good mother tell her child that if she doesn't shut up and behave the whole family will be out on the street again?

I ask, how do cultural norms that assume middle-class material privilege and a stable heterosexual marriage contribute to the marginalization of poor white homeless mothers whose lives deviate from ideologies of "normative" mothering? (Appell 1998; Coontz 1992; Polakow 1993; Kaplan 1997). How does the cultural myth of the sacrificial, devoted, fulfilled, and always motivated mother resonate for women preoccupied with negotiating everyday burdens such as housing, transportation, child care, personal safety, government bureaucracies, and the like? In effect, dominant standards of the good mother readily become another source of injury for mothers whose finances, education, age, living conditions, marital status, and available strategies of solace and escape render such standards out of reach or counterproductive.

My analysis draws on fieldwork conducted in 1994–95 in Portland, Oregon, a medium-sized city in the northwestern United States. There I engaged in ethnographic research, working with homeless mothers at a social service agency, which I will call Westside Community Center (WCC).[1] I selected this population because it epitomizes many of the external markers used to define unfit motherhood, such as poverty, drug addiction, alcoholism, violence in the home, low education levels, youth, marital status, and lack of stable housing. However, my research with homeless mothers is not intended to expand cultural illustrations of "unfit" or "dangerous" mothers. Instead, it attempts to provide a dense description of the lives of mothers who are often used to illustrate irresponsibility, carelessness, and even monstrosity in the domain of mothering.

I conducted my work in a predominantly white urban community. While much research on homelessness has been done in large, more racially diverse urban centers such as New York City, Washington, D.C., and Los Angeles, less attention has been directed at more homogeneous midsize cities.[2] Portland is a city where conservative stereotypes about race, homelessness, and public support collide with the fact that welfare recipients are predominantly white. Poor whites disturb the chain of associations typical in U.S. cultural conceptions of normality, power, and privilege. Such disruptions help keep my research from being uncritically folded into racist narratives about motherhood, poverty, and welfare (Roberts 1991, 1996).

Whiteness constitutes a silent politics in this study. It is mute because unlike women of color who face racist exclusions overtly, impoverished white women are able to deny the ways in which, as Ruth Frankenberg argues, their lives are "racially structured" (Frankenberg 1993). Furthermore, white women are able to identify with what has been imagined as racial normativity (Wray and Newitz 1997). Thus, their difference is often marked more pronouncedly through categories of class and gender. As Matt Wray and Annalee Newitz write in their collection of essays on "white trash":

> White trash is "good to think with" when it comes to issues of race and class in the U.S. because the term foregrounds whiteness and working class or underclass poverty, two social attributes that usually stand far apart in the minds of many Americans, especially American social and cultural theorists. (4)

My work examines the relationships between the lives of the white mothers I studied and cultural norms of mothering. Some of the issues I emphasize would also affect women of color while other issues that would be pronounced in a more diverse community are notably absent. Although it is beyond the scope of this project to adequately interpret those discrepancies, these narratives of white poverty contribute to the changing landscape in our understandings of racial privilege, racial normativity, and racial identifications in general.

This is a study of the cultural imagination of class and gender as it revolves around the lives of mostly white homeless mothers. I examine the women's lives and cultural norms of mothering as a means to question the coherency of marginalized identities. Thus, I explore and interpret the interdependencies and tensions between these lives and norms. I traffic between the life stories offered by the women themselves and their relations to the stories told about them, exploring various resonances, infusions, and tensions among these perspectives. I am interested in the dynamics between the stories people tell about themselves and the stories others tell about them.

The stories I share in the following chapters are not the result of fact-finding missions. They are everyday tales, anecdotes, confessions, and self-dramatizations. Stories are woven together from pieces of the storyteller's memory. I explore meanings in the way that individuals "make" themselves through their stories and define themselves through their positive, negative, or ambiguous responses to the stories told about them. We learn the most from listening to both what people tell us and how they tell it. Sometimes the truths people recall are very important, and sometimes the fictions they insist on are, too.

For example, one of my "clients," Sally, *believes* that the parents she grew up with are not her biological parents or the biological parents of her brothers and sisters. She describes her mother as pretending to be pregnant with each successive child and then buying a baby on the black market. Any family resemblance among siblings is taken by her to be a product of their living so close together.

Now, I do not know whether this is true; indeed, it seems doubtful on the surface. I understand from other parts of Sally's stories that she grew up in a violent and chaotic environment in which she was physically abused and sexually terrorized. These experiences could make her want to dissociate from any biological linkage to her parents. Or her parents may have been involved in some unusual and questionable forms of child procurement. Either way, what is most important to me is not the representational truth of Sally's story but what it reveals about her life and her current identity. That Sally names the man she grew up with her "stepfather" is critical to her identity. That I take her story to reveal a deep dissociation from her parents reflects, I suppose, a doubt on my part about its factual basis. I think she believes it, but I doubt that the belief is well grounded. However, even if the terms of her story shifted significantly, the intensity with which it is told and the signs of disaffection that accompany it are the keys here.

Introduction

In the conclusion of the book *Interpreting Women's Lives* (Barbre et al. 1989), the authors discuss the question of "truth":

> When talking about their lives, people lie sometimes, forget a lot, exaggerate, become confused and get things wrong. Yet they are revealing truths. These truths don't reveal the past "as it actually was" aspiring to a standard of objectivity. They give us instead the truths of our experiences. . . . Unlike the reassuring Truth of the scientific ideal, the truths of personal narratives are neither open to proof nor self-evident. We come to understand them only through interpretation, paying careful attention to the contexts that shape their creation and to the worldviews that inform them. (261)

Sally may or may not reveal her past "as it actually was." Yet she did offer me the opportunity to think about her experiences and the way in which she contextualizes them through the production of a life story.

By working daily with marginalized women, listening to their stories, and intervening officially to help address the difficulties they face, I was in a position to interview them with more street awareness than is often available and to observe some of the dissonances between what they say and what they do. Marginal mothers are neither victims nor demons. They struggle within and against difficult social positions that render stability a precarious goal, foresight an ambiguous good, and responsibility a costly enterprise. My aim is to offer portrayals of mothers in compromising circumstances without sanitizing their lives or ignoring the pain they suffer and engender. And I seek to do so without pretending that I can find an uncompromised position from which to pursue this research.

Indeed, I was in a compromising situation when I conducted my anthropological fieldwork. I was hired at Westside Community Center, a local nonprofit social service agency, as a parent/child specialist in the homeless family program there. I later changed positions to case manager in the same program. In interesting ways my position at the agency immersed me in the worlds of both social workers and clients.

Social workers were my colleagues, my teachers, and my subjects of inquiry. Staff members were aware of my academic pursuits but for the most part were not particularly interested in them.[3] However, like most people with highly cultivated skills, they were often anxious to share their philosophies and analyses. And I was anxious to engage them, both for my immediate survival in this new workplace and for my extended interpretive project. It helped to have two agendas. First, I was able to learn the ropes more quickly and intimately than I might have otherwise. And second, my engagement interrupted the detached perspective that typifies some interpretive work. Since I worked at the agency, I could not, for example, dismiss established social service ideologies and practices without putting something else in their place.

Homeless mothers were designated as my clients, and I will refer to them as such throughout this work. The social service setting provided an institutional backdrop that allowed me to meet and work closely with a wide range of families. My professional position gave me a framework for talking to women and children. My institutional responsibilities also helped channel my abilities into a service that might be useful to individuals.

Of course, such a stance constitutes a danger as well as an opportunity. I was in a position of authority over clients and of accountability to staff. Some may argue that such a position limits what you can learn or even that it is unethical to use it in this way. But any position, institutional or not, limits and shapes what you learn. This is always an issue to acknowledge and address. Additionally, there was the danger of becoming so immersed in current social service models that I would not be able to place them in a larger context. My sense, however, is that these risks can be reduced through the processes of situational self-reflection that an anthropological perspective encourages. And that the connections and tensions between enacting what you interpret and interpreting what you enact contain positive possibilities within them. My ambiguous position (as worker and researcher) allowed me to get more deeply and continuously involved with clients and staff than might otherwise have been the case. The ambiguity of that position also gave me an opportunity to think critically about the role of a staff member in such a setting.

Social services provide a pivotal site for the study of homeless families because they are places where social care and cultural control coexist uneasily. Furthermore, they provide settings where both clients and professionals regularly engage in cultural reflection and self-scrutiny (Skoll 1992; Liebow 1993; Hirsch 1989). In the following chapters, I negotiate my dual positionality in pursuit of a cultural analysis of impoverished and unhoused mothers, of social service practices and identities, and of the cultural stories told about each. Such an analysis, I hope, offers a window into the lives of women some might prefer to leave voiceless, as well as into the ideologies and practices that regulate them.

1. Kristy: A Narrative

When I first met Kristy, early in my stay at Westside Community Center (WCC), I thought she was a drug addict. She was sitting in the day shelter of WCC perched in a chair near a radio that was always on too loud. Her dyed blond hair needed to be washed and was pulled back in a ponytail except for the few strands that fell around her face. She was thin, wearing tight blue jeans and a white crop top. Her eyes were tired and her hands shook as she was introduced to me by Jenny, her case manager.

Kristy was friendly; she also seemed frazzled and unfocused. I sat down carefully in one of the broken rocking chairs—if you leaned back too far, they would topple over—and asked her how she was doing. "Okay, I guess," she answered and laughed that nervous laugh that I would come to know so well over the next few months. Kristy's laugh is, among other things, a coping strategy. She reflects on her life and laughs in disbelief.

With all the curiosity of an energetic five-year-old, Kristy's daughter, Sue Ellen, came over to investigate this new person talking to her mom. Sue Ellen was a slight blond girl with a quick smile and feminine mannerisms that mirrored her mother's. Kristy reprimanded her for the interruption. "Go play," she commanded the little girl, motioning to the other side of the shelter where a small play area was filled with not-so-clean and often less-than-perfect toys. Not entirely deterred, Sue Ellen tried other tactics of bringing the toys near us in order to be closer to the action. But Kristy kept sending her away brusquely. Finally, Sue Ellen gave up, pretending to be engaged with a toy designed for a younger child and looking over at us wistfully from time to time.

"Go play" was a command I heard often during my time at WCC. It expresses the irony of a child's entertainment and imagination translated into a chore. "Go play" often reflects a parent's need for privacy and peace rather than the child's need for playful expression. So I was in a familiar dilemma. I wanted Sue Ellen to feel included, to hear kind words, and to get the extra support and attention that homeless children need as they negotiate uncertainties with their families. Yet to suggest that she might stay with us would not only conflict with Kristy's parenting but would also immediately create a distance between Kristy and me. For what I said in that setting was seldom received as a mere suggestion. Kristy was on my territory, a land where I was the professional. Perhaps Kristy was trying to show that her daughter minds her and is well behaved. Perhaps Kristy needed a break from her daughter or wanted an adult conversation that she felt Sue Ellen should not hear.

I did not know Kristy well enough to interpret her dynamic with her daughter. So I did what I often do at the beginning: unless the conduct is overtly abusive, I let it go. Then I made sure that before I left the shelter Sue Ellen got at least five minutes of my undivided attention, producing as it did with many of the children I saw a rather close attachment built up over a short time. Soon, whenever Sue Ellen saw me she would call out my name, run to give me a big hug, and seek out more of my attention.

Kristy's fidgeting and irritability suggested drug abuse to me as did a few other indicators I saw later, such as the shiny new low-rider convertible truck that her boyfriend drove and their stories about a motorboat and new furniture that her ex-husband's relatives had allegedly stolen. Such possessions are uncommon for a homeless family on welfare. Drug money comes and goes; it often becomes congealed in those flashy possessions that serve as counterpoints to financial instability and homelessness.

But as Kristy and I worked together and became closer, closer than I typically became with clients, it seemed less likely that drugs were a major issue in her life. As with many clients who entered our program, Kristy was scared, uncomfortable, and frustrated at finding herself in this position. When I met her, she was depressed. This depression showed in her anxious mannerisms, which could easily have been mistaken for signs of drug use. Furthermore, their notable possessions amid homelessness, rather than indicating involvement in the drug industry, instead were the result of her partner's sporadic employment and an inability to budget adequately. Thus my initial impressions, ideas, and concerns upon meeting Kristy could easily have led me in a different direction. But Kristy's story was more complex. Kristy's story, like the stories of other women I worked with, complicates and distorts welfare categories that might otherwise be applied to her. Over the next several months Kristy revealed pieces and chunks of her life to me. I offer some of those fragments here, to allow some of the twists and turns in one woman's life to stand out a little more sharply.

Kristy was born in 1969, making her twenty-six when we met—exactly my age. She was born in Portland and lived with both of her parents until she was eight years old. Her parents owned a small restaurant as well as two homes, one of which they rented out.

Kristy's parents separated when she was eight and her younger sister, June, was two. Her mother quickly became involved romantically with one of her coworkers, making Kristy wonder if she had been having an affair before the separation. Her father had had frequent affairs throughout the marriage. Soon Kristy's mother, along with her two daughters, moved in with the new boyfriend, Nick.

Nick was an alcoholic. "He tried. He was actually a good stepfather role model except for the alcohol part," Kristy said. He would regularly come home late at night drunk, sometimes prompting fights between him and her mother.

Over the next several years the new family moved numerous times, first to a small town in rural Washington, then to Nebraska, and then to Idaho. While her mom initially had steady work in Portland at a store where she was promoted a couple of times, as they moved, her jobs became more sporadic, paying less money. This downward mobility and frequent change of residences almost certainly had effects on their home life.

Kristy did not disclose any physical abuse during her childhood. She described her mother as "always being there," and her discussion of chores and a regular allowance suggested a fairly stable family life. While it is clear that Kristy's childhood was not idyllic, it was apparently not marked by significant violence. This is significant because observers often conclude that the common occurrence of violence and chaos in the histories of homeless women is directly linked to their economic predicaments. But the rough correlation between economic position, violence, and homelessness may in fact mask the multiple ways in which people's lives become unstable.

Kristy was living in Idaho when she started high school. She liked school well enough and believed she could have done well if she had attended regularly. However, Kristy started to ditch school to have more time to hang out with her girlfriends. When Kristy was sixteen years old, she started running away. She would disobey her mother and then stay at a friend's house for a couple of days until her mom found her and took her home. Kristy's mother assumed she was out sleeping with boys, but Kristy contends that boys were not a major part of the equation at that point. She went on birth control pills at her mother's insistence but claims it was unnecessary, since she was not sexually active.

One time after Kristy ran off with her friends, her mother called the police and reported her as a runaway. "The police picked me up and put me in jail!" Kristy laughed, her eyes wide with disbelief. She was sent to family court. Her mom called Kristy "out of control" and told the judge that she "couldn't handle her." The judge ordered Kristy to go to a boarding school designed for girls in trouble.

Kristy said most of the girls in the school were there for things like alcohol and drug abuse or sexual promiscuity. She claimed that these were never issues for her and that the school assessed her problem as "rebelliousness." Kristy loved the school, which she described as based on a "counseling model." She liked the "structure" of her everyday life there the most. She attended for one year until she graduated.

After receiving her diploma, Kristy moved back to Portland where her mom and her sister had returned to live. Her mom had by now separated from Nick and was living with Kristy's paternal grandmother. Kristy's grandmother maintained close relationships with her grandchildren, facilitating visits back to Portland when they lived out of state and remembering birthdays, holidays, and so on. Kristy felt she could count on her grandmother, saying, for instance, that when her release date from school was approaching, she knew that at least her grandmother would help her get back to Portland. Of course, this also suggests that her faith in her parents was quite limited.

Kristy's grandmother tried to encourage a relationship between her son and his children:

> So she'd see to it that she'd send us a bus ticket or money for a bus ticket every summer for a couple weeks to come down to see her but also to make it like to see him, too. But I know it was mostly her. If it hadn't been for her doing that, he wouldn't have did it. Not because he doesn't love us or didn't, you know what I mean? Just 'cause. She would always send us birthday cards and sign his name on them. I know. It didn't fool me. [Kristy laughs that laugh.]

So with her diploma in hand, Kristy moved back to Portland into her grandmother's house with her mom and sister, and looked around for a job:

> I had never, ever thought about what I wanted to do. You know how some people know what they want to do—they want to be a cop, or a doctor, or a social worker. I had never thought about it. I think I wanted to just be a millionaire or something. I don't know how I was gonna get there. Maybe I was gonna marry one or something. I don't know. Or maybe I wanted to be a bum. [She laughs.]

Neither of Kristy's parents graduated from college, although she remembers her mom taking an occasional community college class. And college was not in the picture for Kristy: "I could tell. I mean, it was like . . . obvious . . . that there was no bank account, you know, open for my college fund or anything." She laughed. So Kristy took a job working at a local snack bar, Rudy's, where she wore a "dorky" uniform. She did not voice any other complaints about the work.

Through her sister she met a man from California, Tim,

who was living in the neighborhood with relatives. She began spending time with him: "Not really dating or anything, but I'd go with him to auto parts stores . . . or we'd walk all the kids [his relatives] to the school and watch them play . . . and then I started really liking him a lot."

It was not long before Kristy moved with Tim to his hometown in California. Kristy was reluctant to make the move. She liked Portland, and Tim's rural hometown was very small and made up "mostly" of Tim's relatives. Kristy never fully explained why she decided to move in spite of her ambivalence. It may be a marker that she did not feel in control of her life, but instead that life was something that happened to her. The couple lived with Tim's parents, who were very strict about their not sleeping together outside of marriage. In spite of this rule, Kristy found herself pregnant a couple months later. She had not been using birth control:

> I guess I just figured I wouldn't get pregnant. I don't know. I had never got pregnant before and I had never used birth control. . . . I had only slept with maybe four people before Tim. . . . But so here we are in California and now I'm pregnant and that's just an awful sin 'cause we're not married and we're not supposed to be sleeping together. You know, "How did you get pregnant?" . . . His older sister, they had this great big huge wedding planned . . . and then all of a sudden one day it's, "Cancel the wedding. We got to go to Las Vegas and get married today," and they left like that weekend . . . and got married. And then like nine months later she had a baby [laughs]. But she won't ever admit to this day that they slept together before they were married, if you ask her or her mom.

Kristy also got married in Las Vegas when she was five months pregnant. She had not really thought about marriage before this:

> No, it wasn't even in the plan. I never really even thought about marriage. In fact, the whole time I was growing up I was never gonna get married. Me and all my friends ran around saying, "We're never gonna get married, we're never gonna have any kids." You know? . . . We [she and Tim] decided, well, we'll go get married. Whatever makes everybody happy or whatever. Well, we loved each other and stuff, too, so it wasn't like you're gonna marry someone you hate. It wasn't a bad thing. So we did it.

Kristy's lack of interest in marriage is intriguing. In some ways her discussion of "not really having contemplated it" suggests a general lack of forethought evident in other parts of her story. However, her earlier aversion to marriage may mark a desire for independence and a break from traditional expectations. Kristy appeared at first glance to conform to familiar feminine stereotypes. And yet she rejected the future image of herself as a wife, preferring instead to bond with girl peers in search of something different.

Kristy got married at the Silver Bells Chapel in Las Vegas. For $99 a limousine picked them up at the hotel and took them to the ceremony. Tim's family accompanied them but Kristy's did not. Kristy wore a white gown with a long train that she bought at a resale store. She described her situation with her typical humor:

> We got married at like noon and I wore that. Here I am five months pregnant with this big huge [motions to her belly and laughs] . . . and I'm going into all the casinos all day until like midnight that night. I'm only eighteen and I'm gambling on all the poker machines and no one's asking me for ID or nothing.

Kristy and Tim continued living with his parents, which was a real struggle for Kristy. She described them as "Neanderthals"—the women were expected to serve the men at all times. Kristy had a hard time getting used to the subservience and the constant criticisms she received from Tim's mother. So she and Tim moved back and forth between California and Portland periodically, never putting down roots in either place: "I was married to him for five years, and we probably went back and forth between Portland and California at least twenty times."

Kristy had recently returned to Portland when she went into labor. She had just arrived with her whole family at her grandfather's funeral. She was getting out of the car at the cemetery:

> I was in jeans and high heels, nine months pregnant [we laugh together at this image]. . . . I stood up and all of a sudden my water broke, which I didn't know that's what happened at the time . . . and I'm crying—the instant thing was just to cry. I started crying, and I was all warm and wet, and I'm just crying. And so here's my mom like, "Don't cry, it's okay. Just sit down." And I'm like, "No." It's all gushy feeling, it's like warm and it feels sticky and it's in my shoes and it's everywhere. I'm like, "I don't want to get it on your car." You know?

No one remained to attend the funeral. Instead, they all piled back into the cars and drove Kristy to the hospital. Kristy had been seeing a doctor regularly in California but did not feel connected with her new doctor in Portland: "He was a senile old man, real old, old, old. I couldn't believe he was my doctor, 'cause he was so old. I thought he should be retired or something."

Her doctor had not explained to her what would happen when she went into labor. Childbirth shocked and scared Kristy. She was in labor for thirty-six hours but was unable to deliver the baby vaginally. She gave birth through an emergency cesarean section. When I asked her if she had known about cesarean births previously, she answered, "I knew as much as I knew about natural childbirth—nothing." Kristy had a nine-pound boy whom they named Jonathan Ross after his paternal grandfather. They call him JR. Soon after his birth they drove back to California in spite of the doctor's warnings that the baby was too young for such a long trip.

Kristy's life in California was somewhat unfocused. She and Tim moved around a lot, sometimes living with his parents, sometimes living with a cousin of Tim's and his girlfriend (Susie) and their four children in hotels or apartments. Kristy loved living with this other couple. She was very close with Susie, who shared Kristy's disdain for the "backward hillbilly" ways of Tim's extended family:

> I would have rather lived with them than not down there. . . .
> I mean, you know, it was like much more fun. We all woke up
> every morning, and me and Susie would cook breakfast and
> feed all six of our little kids, and you know, we'd go to the
> park . . . or to the river . . . or wherever. If it was just me and
> Tim and the kids, it probably would have been different. Tim
> probably woulda slept all day . . . and the kids and me would
> have just been laying there watching TV or something. So it
> was like company, always someone to be with. . . . I can tell
> you I never got sick of her and she never got sick of me, as far
> as I could tell. I'm sure it was a mutual thing.
>
> We'd always talk about, "God, how did we end up like
> this?" 'cause they [the men] were so weird. They'd be like,
> "Get me a glass of water," . . . and sometimes you're like, "Get
> your own water," you know what I mean? Or, "You get me
> some."

Kristy's bond with her cousin-in-law was one of the ways she coped with a marriage she felt stuck in. Susie was her companion, and she never tired of her company. She got sick of Tim and his arbitrary demands.

In this way Kristy represents a new kind of feminism, although I doubt she would use this name. She believes that Tim expects her to be subservient because he exists in an unsophisticated and backward world where such traditions are maintained. She distinguishes herself and Susie (who is originally from a big city in California) from such modes, explaining that they are beyond such ancient ideologies. In Kristy's mind, she and Susie are more "up to style," and that progressivism includes certain feminist ideologies even if they are not categorized as such.

But Kristy did adapt to certain aspects of rural California life. She says her kids were always filthy because the environment was so dusty; she allowed them to run around naked looking like "rug rats" even though she would never permit this in the more sophisticated city of Portland. She also adopted the expected lifestyle of a nonworking mother though she maintained a certain distance from it in her commentaries:

> We were all on welfare, you know? No one was working. . . .
> None of them [Tim's family] worked. His mom, they all draw
> disability. In California it's so easy to get disability or be on
> welfare. All you have to do is pretend like you're retarded or
> an alcoholic or illiterate. If you're illiterate, you can get like
> $600–$700 a month just for not knowing how to read or
> write or spell—and how they gonna know if you really know
> and you're just saying you don't? . . . Everybody down there
> was like that, getting some check for something or other. . . .
> So all this government and state money is everywhere down
> there. The first and the third and the fifth [of the month] all
> these checks are rolling in, you know? And plus to live on wel-
> fare is $824. Why would you want to work? I mean, you get all
> your medical insurance—that's for all three of us—paid. You
> get $200–$300 in food stamps to buy your food with. . . .
> Rent's cheap. . . . Like one time . . . somehow we decided to

go to Magic Mountain instead of paying our rent. So we ended up having to move. We all went to Magic Mountain and Disneyland, and you know, we just took off for a couple weeks and did irresponsible things all the time. We always did.

One of the reasons I was surprised by how Kristy discussed Tim's family and the welfare system was that I had been lumping multiple codes of morality together. Since the family was adamantly against premarital sex and held conservative views on marriage and gender roles, I somehow assumed that such a position would be tied to other mainstream notions of responsible behavior, such as a work ethic, the stability of home, and opposition to welfare. However, what felt like a conflict to me did not feel so contradictory to this family. Or perhaps these very paradoxes are what make such a logic prevalent and appealing. One response to feeling marginalized by ethical doctrines about work that do not reflect one's life is to compensate by endorsing other moral codes about sexuality and male dominance.

Kristy embodies some of the contradictions in recent welfare debates. On one hand, she is somewhat critical of those who cheat the system. However, she simultaneously criticizes the system, suggesting that it lends itself to fraudulence. Finally, she herself is caught up in the system, relying on it instead of traditional forms of employment. Kristy suggests that her behavior had "irresponsible" elements, but she also shows us in other parts of her story that such irresponsibility needs to be read in a context of struggle and youthful confusion.

Kristy often describes welfare in the terms that its opponents use. She knows that it has drawbacks and self-defeating dimensions. But her critical words are delivered in a light-hearted tone—a tone that suggests another understanding of the background from which the welfare life emerges and against which her descriptions of its travails are set. For example, her discussion of how "easy" it is to get welfare is set against a backdrop of how hard it is to get a stable, well-paying job if you have a limited education and lack established family connections to fall back on when things are tough. Her laughter about the trip to Disneyland expresses both the element of ridiculousness in it and an appreciation of the need for temporary release from their overwhelming problems. Perhaps she suspects that most people will miss the second element unless they themselves encounter those circumstances. Perhaps she also knows that unless you see ways to break out of a settled pattern of instability, you are likely to succumb to the demand for temporary release. Kristy does not sanitize her life on welfare. Indeed, she invokes some of the values her opponents use against her. Still, she does so in ways that can call the sufficiency of those judgments into question.

Fifteen months after Kristy gave birth to JR, she had her second child, Sue Ellen. (While she denies that she named them after the notorious couple from the nighttime soap opera *Dallas,* the kids often cite those characters as their namesakes.) This time she gave birth in California and again had a C-section. She describes that experience as particularly traumatic because she went into labor a month early and then was anesthetized against her will for the procedure instead of being allowed to watch with mirrors as she had done with JR: "They told me—they didn't ask me—they told me, 'You're going to sleep now.' And I was like, 'No! No!' I was crying, 'No! No!' and then it's only like one or two breaths into that thing and you're out. . . . There wasn't no choice."

Sue Ellen had to stay in the hospital nursery for three weeks. Kristy spent one of them in the hospital with her and the other two she drove the thirty miles up three times a day to feed and hold her. Kristy said quietly, "It was sad, and I cried all the time. The whole time I cried a lot."

When Sue Ellen was released from the hospital, they all moved in with Tim's parents again. She, Tim, and Sue Ellen shared a bedroom converted from the dining room, and JR had a small room of his own. A week after Sue Ellen was home, Tim's parents received a call from his sister who lived outside of town, saying she had been robbed of everything she owned. Tim's parents left to spend the night with their daughter, leaving just Kristy, Tim, Tim's younger sister, and the children in the house:

> That night at like two or three in the morning it was hot, and I was so tired just from everything. It was only a week, Sue Ellen just got home from the hospital, and I'm just laying there hot. . . . Finally, I'm going, "Shit! I'm gonna open the door or something." And I get up and there's fire everywhere. I open my eyes and the whole house is on fire! JR's room is in the front, but he had woke up crying in the middle of the night before that happened, so I'd let him [sleep] right by our bed. . . . The fire's like maybe three feet from us. . . . So I just start screaming at the top of my lungs. I didn't have no clothes on. I had a shirt on with no underwear, and I don't have time to be looking for any. I got the kids with no clothes. . . . Tim wears contacts and he can't see worse than Sue Ellen. . . . We're just trying to get out of the house. We opened the sliding glass door and ran out and sat JR down on the ground. He's probably a year or so old, and so he's crying or whatever he's doing. I ran back in and grabbed Sue Ellen and now we're all standing out there and I'm like, "Tim, you know your sister's in there." So he went running in there and caught his face on fire and his hair and opened that door and she jumped out her window.

Everyone escaped the fire; Tim suffered minor burns. But the house burned down, and nothing was salvaged from it. So the entire family had to start from scratch with no personal possessions. Kristy was especially distressed about losing a whole set of new baby furniture she had just received from a shower for Sue Ellen. The Red Cross put them up in a motel until they were able to find an apartment.

Kristy and Tim's relationship deteriorated rapidly after the fire. They fought more often and bitterly, and he became more domineering toward her—trying to "send her to her room" whenever she did something he didn't like. One time the fighting became violent. Tim hit her several times and physically prevented her from leaving. When he fell asleep, she escaped and got help from a neighbor. She had Tim arrested and was planning to go to a women's domestic violence shelter and press charges against him. But his parents intervened and convinced her to try to work things out.

At the same time, Sue Ellen, who was only two months old, grew increasingly sick and began losing weight, vomiting, and having frequent diarrhea. Kristy took Sue Ellen to the hospital. Sue Ellen was admitted for ten days, and they diagnosed her as dehydrated and severely allergic to formula. The hospital staff berated Kristy for not bringing her in earlier. Kristy stayed with Sue Ellen in the hospital, sleeping in a chair she folded out at night.

After Sue Ellen was released, Tim and Kristy fell back together again and moved back to Portland. They began working through temporary employment agencies. Tim's job turned into permanent full-time. Kristy returned to her old job at the snack bar working part time.

For a while they made a go of it, living in an apartment in Portland and earning a steady income. Soon Kristy and Tim began "hanging around a bunch of people that were into drugs real bad, and that's when he [Tim] started using drugs and started shooting drugs intravenously." Tim denied using speed to both his employer and Kristy when they questioned him. But Kristy was not fooled:

I'm not an idiot. I've seen too many people on it. So I kept
telling him if you don't quit it, I'm gonna leave. . . . He did
weird things when he knew I was getting ready to leave. . . . He
could tell. I wouldn't sleep with him anymore, or if he tried,
I'd go to the couch or whatever. . . . And he'd do weird things
like he'd dig my wedding dress out of my cedar chest and he'd
lay it on the bed and set the Bible on top of it. [She laughs.]
You know, . . . that's weird. I mean, that's been packed away
and . . . I'd be like, "Please, that ain't gonna help, and it's kinda
psycho." It ain't something normal people do. . . . And finally
I just left.

Kristy moved with her children into her mother's house in
Portland. Tim continued to harass her, calling and coming
over repeatedly after she asked him to leave her alone. Sometimes he would hide in the bushes, waiting for her to leave
work. "I know he was on drugs then, too, because you know,
why would he be in the bushes?" She eventually got a re-
straining order against him when he would not stop following her.

Kristy worried that Tim's family might press him to seek
custody of the kids, so at first she did not let him see them at
all after the separation. She felt his attempts to see the children were merely excuses to see her: "I'm a good mother. I'm
better than Tim is at taking care of the kids. . . . In the re-
straining order he was not allowed anywhere around me
or the kids, so there wasn't no reason for him to see the kids."

The divorce Kristy got through Legal Aid took nearly a
year. The lawyers walked her through the process and encouraged her to file for full custody, giving Tim only supervised
visitation:

I wanted to give him more . . . just because I thought that was
right. You know, right from wrong. I don't know, I just figure
most dads . . . I mean, a lot of dads probably aren't like him,

using drugs or whatever. But you know, you see a lot of dads get their kids on the weekends, and mom has them during the week or whatever, or even every other weekend. But they didn't think that was a good idea. You know, the lady that was talking me through the divorce papers.

Kristy is torn between wanting her children to have a relationship with their dad, even though his drug use goes against the moral codes of child safety that the Legal Aid worker supports. People on my side of the desk are very often torn over this issue, too. We usually come down on the side Kristy resists.

When I met Kristy a couple years after the divorce, she was handling this contradiction by ignoring the legal agreement. She felt guilty about it but still continued to do it. Tim was still using drugs, she suspected, but she allowed the children to go on unsupervised visits with him anyway, when he occasionally got it together to keep a scheduled visit. She said she worried about them when they were with him and that sometimes one of the children, usually Sue Ellen, would call her and beg to come home early. Still, she felt it was important for them to know their father. Besides, sometimes this was her only way to get a break, a problem that poor single mothers frequently face.

During one of our first conversations, before I knew much about her, Kristy told me about her ex-husband's addiction and the sporadic pattern of his visits with the children. I began discussing the importance of not allowing them to be with him unsupervised, suggesting a variety of ways to do this. I detected a glazed look in Kristy's eyes. But I was too involved in the issue as I recognized it to pursue this point. As it turns out, she had heard my kind of line several times before. It spoke to only one dimension of her life while sliding over other elements of it. Kristy knows her situation pretty well.

She also knows when our plans for her are not likely to work very well or for very long. Listening to me has sometimes been an exercise in patience for her.

Eventually, after her separation Kristy moved into her own apartment with her children. Her younger sister, June, moved in with them, sleeping on the couch. June became Kristy's live-in babysitter. Kristy worked temporary jobs and began going out to bars: "I'm going out all the time, dancing. I mean, Wednesday, Thursday, Friday, Saturday, sometimes 'til two or three o'clock in the morning and getting up and going to work the next day.... I'd never been to bars before.... I was married when I turned twenty-one, and that wasn't one of the things Tim did."

Kristy's life began to revolve around her social world. She did not see any men seriously at first. She worried about what her children would think if they woke up in the morning and there was a strange man in her bed. But soon a friend introduced Kristy to Joe. His ex-wife had killed herself, and their daughter was living with her grandmother. Joe was seeing another woman at the time. He hid this fact from Kristy at first. But he broke it off with that woman when Kristy began seeing him more seriously.

Joe had been in jail for "a few different things—assault, I know that." When I asked Kristy if his criminal record made her nervous, she shook her head: "Uh-uh, no. It didn't bother me. I didn't know all the things that he'd been in trouble for up front, but it still didn't bother me. And I had never been out with anyone either that was a criminal . . . or an ex-criminal, or whatever you want to call it." In fact, Kristy displays a sense of intrigue or excitement about Joe's past. On the weekends, she liked driving to the coast, where Joe performed his community service. She would wait for him to finish his work, hanging out in a trailer that a relative loaned them. Then they would go for walks or drives together: "That was kinda neat. I always looked forward to it. I don't know if he did, picking up trash or whatever he did."

Kristy and Joe moved in together, changing residences a couple times before moving into a rental owned by a friend of Joe's. Joe worked off and on for the landlord, doing yard and maintenance work. But after they'd lived in this place for a few months, the owner/friend put it up for sale and told them they would have to move out. While the landlord had promised to give Kristy and Joe at least a month's notice, he reneged on that promise, and they were forced to leave in a matter of days. Kristy said they had a lease and that she probably could have fought him in court. But she felt that "it would have been a hassle for everyone involved, and I don't have the money to be taking anybody to court."

Kristy remembered that after the house fire Red Cross had helped them with a motel voucher while they searched for a new place to live. She called them this time, too, and was directed to a number of social service agencies, eventually getting an appointment at WCC. Kristy perhaps did not realize she was lucky to get an appointment. WCC turns away nine out of ten callers because of its full caseload.

When Joe drove Kristy to the appointment, she had him wait in the truck and told WCC staff that he was a friend who had just given her a ride. Kristy assumed that she could only get help if she were a single mother with no romantic attachments. AFDC (Aid to Families with Dependent Children) rules have taught Kristy that having a significant partner may make her ineligible for social assistance.

The agency building is fairly nondescript, set on a busy road in Portland. It is one story high with a few low-level windows protected by iron bars. The main entrance opens into a short, dark hallway that holds two bathrooms, one kept locked for staff because, as the director, Margaret, a white woman in her midthirties, told me, "I like to know who I'm sharing my bathroom with." There were also two big cupboards in which food donations were stored before distribution to clients. The cupboards changed from bare to full regularly, but the items never varied much: banged-up cans of beans or vegetables, instant soup mixes, discontinued products, cereals, and jars of various sauces. If the kids were lucky, there was peanut butter and jelly, but bread was rare.

The receptionist, Justin, is a white man in his early sixties, with an offbeat sense of humor. He is friendly and warm. He knows poverty firsthand, having been homeless himself at one point. Justin is now very careful with his money, never, for example, treating himself to a lunch out, but instead heating up a can of soup. He takes the bus to and from work. He worries about his future finances when he retires.

Three or four student-type chairs with desks attached to them—the kind that is consistently uncomfortable—sit in front of him. Here, Kristy waited for her first meeting with her new case manager, Jenny, a well-meaning white woman in her midtwenties. Beyond this there are two offices, occupied by two or three workers each. There are also additional cubicles for more workers. Kristy met with Jenny in the intake room, which is the only place in the office for confidential conversations with clients or staff. It has a sagging couch, a long desk with a couple of chairs, and a bin with a few random toys for children during the sometimes long meetings with their parents.

The most active space in the agency is the day shelter. There is a small kitchen with a sink and a dish rack (frequently containing dirty dishes), a microwave that works moderately, and a fridge. There is a round table for eating and hanging out. Then there is a children's area, a corner of the room with shelves strewn with some toys. These toys are often dirty, sometimes broken, and not always safe for the wide range of ages of kids who have access to them.

There is a phone available for client use. There is also a daily newspaper for clients to go through the classifieds. There is no television, because the staff worried that clients would just sit around and watch it rather than getting other things done. Two offices border this room, both with glass fronts looking into the day shelter, and neither with walls flush to the ceiling; these were likely the loudest and least private offices. One was occupied by the drug and alcohol specialist, Miranda, a white woman in her late forties, and shared by a woman who ran the energy assistance program. The other was shared by me, when I was the parent/child specialist, and the day shelter monitor/program assistant, Barry, a Black man in his midthirties.

For me, this office took some getting used to, as did the day shelter for clients. It was sometimes intensely loud, especially during the winter months when the cold and rain filled the small room with twenty or so children, parents, and staff bustling around. Because you can see into my office, both clients and children imagine I am constantly available; the endless interruptions make it hard to conduct meetings or complete other work. I had splitting headaches by the end of each day for the first few weeks. For clients, the day shelter sometimes feels like a fishbowl. They are constantly in the company of others and have no privacy. They also have nowhere else to go. So it is a mixed blessing of sorts.

After Kristy was introduced to the program and shown around, she was vouchered into a motel.[1] Kristy allowed Joe to stay there with her at the motel and was immediately confronted by her case manager, Jenny, who had been called by the motel manager. Kristy confessed that Joe was a serious and permanent boyfriend. Jenny said she should have told her from the beginning but agreed to add him to the case plan the next week.

The agency expects its clients to show a high level of trust toward workers from the start. But Kristy did not know the program, the philosophies behind it, or any staff or clients. She was in a desperate situation, in need of immediate help, and she knew that she might be denied help if she said or did the wrong thing. She just does not always know exactly what the wrong thing is.

However, even while WCC staff are aware of these constraints, they have reasons for demanding that clients be square with them. Realistic understanding of client circumstances is essential to the development of a good case plan. So while Jenny agreed to add Joe to the caseload, she also insisted on waiting until the next week and asked Kristy not to allow him to stay with her until then. Kristy was being given another chance, but she also had another rule to follow, perhaps to prove that she was willing to follow the rules at all. Kristy continued to have trouble at the motel and felt that the manager treated them unfairly, constantly looking for reasons to complain about them to Jenny. Kristy had the sense that she was being watched constantly. The fact that she was not paying for the room herself heightened her sense of powerlessness:

> The stove didn't work the whole time I was there [and] I never asked [them to fix it]. They were supposed to come in and change the laundry and clean and everything, and I never had them do anything like that, ever. I never bothered them or asked them for anything. . . . And it was like they were always watching us.

The experience of being watched and judged is common for social service clients. It is one of the ways they are regulated and organized. Privacy and autonomy are middle-class luxuries. The dues that the down-and-out pay for assistance are surveillance, regulation, and the reduction of decision-making rights. For example, one Friday afternoon Kristy had a regular appointment with her case manager. At that meeting, Jenny requested that Kristy vacate the motel where they had been living and move into a church shelter that evening. This was the first Kristy had heard of the change. Jenny told Kristy that an opening had come up at one of the church shelters and that she felt it was a better place for her. However, Kristy knew the family leaving the shelter and so she knew that the opening had not just "come up" but that this family, too, was being relocated suddenly. Neither client was clear about why this change was taking place. They discussed it with each other. It affected their wariness toward the agency in general.

From a staff point of view, the transition was arranged to placate professional colleagues. The clients in the church shelter were causing difficulties for shelter volunteers. The mother struggled with parenting and relationship issues, and the volunteers requested that she move on. Simultaneously, the motel manager continued to be frustrated by Kristy and her family and did not want them to stay there. WCC's relationships with shelters and motels are fragile and precious. Staff often feel that they cannot afford to jeopardize this. Sometimes the agency chooses to move individual clients around to maintain the general availability of these spaces, so the switch was arranged. But policies about client confidentiality meant that neither client could hear about the other's situation from their case manager. So both clients were left feeling confused, disoriented, and distrustful. Decisions were being made that they neither participated in nor understood. Furthermore, the very idea of a shelter was foreign and frightening to Kristy:

> Here I am thinking, you know, "Okay, a shelter." Now I'm gonna walk in this room and there's gonna be like cots

everywhere and you know what I mean. . . . And I'm scared to death. I don't want to go and neither does Joe. . . . We're like, "No way." . . . You know, get there at 6:30 P.M. and that's it. You don't leave until the next day at 8:00 A.M., and you're like, "What's gonna happen?" You know there's lots of times I want a Diet Coke at 10:00 P.M. at night or . . . I want to go outside, or Joe wants to go smoke a cigarette at midnight, or who knows?

The certainty of surveillance and regulation and the uncertainty of just how tight they will be often unsettle clients like Kristy. Under conditions of duress these minor pleasures can be very important. The inability to enjoy them also reminds you just how little autonomy you have in a world where freedom is the highest mark of self-dignity.

Joe and Kristy decided they really did not want to go to the shelter. Joe told me later that he had already been in jail and did not want to be "locked down" again. They called to ask what would happen if they just slept in their car instead of going there. Jenny had already gone home for the day. Her supervisor, Sandy, a white woman in her fifties and someone who Kristy felt was always "standoffish," took the call. Sandy said the shelter was "nice" and that they should at least go for the weekend because the shelter was expecting them and had ordered that much food, and so on. Kristy said that this did not reassure or convince her. But still, she was afraid of "burning" the people who were expecting her and burning any bridges she had with the agency.

They went to the shelter. They almost left when the other family staying there had a huge fight. But the night hosts (who were volunteers from the church) eventually got things under control and convinced them to stay. Throughout the time they stayed there Kristy and Joe had trouble with the other homeless family, a young couple and their three-year-old daughter, also WCC clients. They were "loud" and "dirty." Other than that, "I liked it actually. It was neat," Kristy said. They enjoyed the volunteers who came each evening. Kristy told me that when she and Joe became more "stable," they wanted to volunteer there themselves.

Kristy changed a lot over the time I knew her at WCC. I worked with her and Joe and the kids in my role as a parent/child specialist. We met numerous times to discuss parenting issues; I enrolled them in a parenting class we offered at the time. I noted during our meetings that Kristy and Joe had different views and strategies for parenting. I felt that Joe had inappropriately high expectations for the children and less patience than Kristy. But they both seemed genuinely open to suggestions, and the three of us enjoyed an easy and warm rapport.

While I had numerous close relationships with women clients at WCC, the men I worked with were often more challenging for me. I had to ward off feelings of intimidation. Some men would stare me down and/or just ignore me altogether. My own self-confidence and sense of personal safety were sometimes placed in jeopardy. Also, the many cases of domestic violence and child abuse, with men the most frequent perpetrators, made it hard not to make negative assumptions about some male clients early on. While I could let my guard down with women clients and become their confidante, not worrying too much about boundaries, I usually felt much more aware of my verbal and body language with male clients. I was afraid that having a close or warm rapport with male clients might be misinterpreted by them. Thus, I tended to keep a stronger professional distance from men than I did from women or children.

But Joe was the male client with whom I developed the best rapport. Joe is a likable, personable man. He laughed at my jokes and teased me in return, calling me the "hippie peace girl." He was always friendly and easygoing. He took care in the way he dressed and presented himself. I felt so comfortable with him that one time when facing a last-minute cancellation by a child-care volunteer, I asked him to help me out with the evening's child care group. I was confident in my judgment of him.

After Kristy had been in our program a couple of months, her case manager, Jenny, quit and I assumed her position. Kristy and Joe came on my caseload at our mutual request, our having already established a relationship of trust and closeness. Kristy had become one of my favorite clients. She was receiving counseling, had been prescribed Prozac for depression, and seemed to be working actively on her parenting skills. The agitation that marked my first impressions of her was all but erased. Joe had gotten a job. Their financial future looked brighter. They moved into one of our transitional units and were looking for permanent housing. Joe's pay was reasonable, and there was reason to believe they would find housing in the next month or two.

Kristy and I would often sit and chat in the day shelter if schedules permitted. We had things in common and I enjoyed Kristy's spirit. She would show up in her convertible low-rider truck, a diet soda in her hand, wearing a crop top and jean shorts and looking more like she was in a Pepsi commercial than at a social service agency. I had to fight with myself to keep "boundaries" (a catchall phrase at WCC, indicating a professional code of distance) around the friendship. The client-staff lines were not dissolved between us, and we spent most of our time working on her "issues." But she also took an interest in my life, asking about my boyfriend, why I did not have kids (a favorite question of my clients to me), about my previous life in California, and so on. Their transitional unit was only several blocks from my own home, and sometimes I felt tempted to invite the family over for a barbecue. I never did, but the boundaries were not always clear.

I was also attached to Kristy's children. They came to my children's groups in the evenings, jumped on me in the day shelter when they could, and shared stories with me. I worked with Kristy to get Sue Ellen glasses (she is extremely near-sighted) and to find strategies for keeping this five-year-old girl wearing them. We also strategized about helping Sue Ellen to not wet her pants, which was becoming a more frequent problem after years of being potty trained. Joe believed she was just being lazy and would stop if punished severely enough. I argued that it was probably stress and that they needed to be relaxed and casual about it. I also attributed JR's frequent diarrhea and stomachaches to stress. But then, I did not know the whole story.

Months after I started working with Joe and Kristy, I went on a routine scheduled home visit to their transitional housing unit. The tension was palpable when I walked in the door. Joe was sitting on the couch, glowering. Kristy was flying around the apartment, visibly agitated and turning the place upside down looking for something. Joe said hello to me, but there was none of the friendliness and lightness that I had come to expect. Kristy said nothing, continuing to upset piles of clothes and search through cupboards and the fireplace. Joe said she was looking for a set of keys to the truck. But these seemed unlikely places for keys.

"This happens every day," Joe told me, referring to Kristy's misplacing of things. And then suddenly came a river of shouting.

"Well, leave then," Kristy screamed at him. "No one's making you stay here."

Then he was in her face, the very proximity of his body pushing her onto the couch. He was yelling at her, spitting words that she was "slipping," that she was "losing her mind," and that he couldn't "deal with it anymore."

"I'm leaving," he hissed and grabbed a pack of Camels and a five dollar bill. He turned to me as I stood in the entryway uncertainly and snarled, "Have a nice day, Debbie," storming out and speeding off in his truck.

I breathed a sigh of relief as he departed, grateful that he'd left and that the kids were outside playing.

Kristy was sobbing on the couch. I sat down next to her, rubbing her arm, and let her gather herself. I turned off the television, which was driving me crazy, adding to the racket in my mind. I knew that Kristy, like most clients I worked with, would never turn it off herself. Perhaps the noise of an unwatched television is less disruptive to them than the turbulence in their everyday lives. More likely, it is comforting.

Kristy's story came pouring out with her tears. Kristy had tried to leave Joe more than ten times in the two years they had been together. Each time he had pursued her, sometimes convincing her to come back to him with promises of change. Sometimes, as she put it, he would "kidnap" her, keeping her with him until she would finally consent to stay. He consistently told her that she was lazy, stupid, and incompetent. He hit her on numerous occasions. She showed me pictures of her purple and black body from a time when Joe forced her out of a moving truck. "He didn't even stop after," she told me. It was the neighbors who came and brought her to the hospital.

"But the worst thing," Kristy sobbed, "is what Joe does to the kids." She continued through her tears:

> He constantly belittles them, screaming that they are stupid, retarded, ugly, freaks, and that he hates them. He tells JR I don't love him, only his younger sister. He screams until the children are paralyzed with fear, and sometimes Sue Ellen

pees all over herself and JR ends up on the toilet with diarrhea from the knots in his stomach. He threatens both of them with physical violence. . . . Sometimes, when he's yelling at them, they look up at me like, "Why don't you protect us?"

Joe's previous comments during our meetings started haunting my brain—about how Kristy was too soft on the kids, how she favored Sue Ellen, and how she spoiled both of them. I remembered discussing with them the importance of backing each other up, of not undermining the other's disciplinary codes. Did I play a part in Kristy's silence, in her not protecting her children from his abuse? How had I not sensed this coming? I've recognized this very early in other families. But not here. I don't know why I missed it. Perhaps my closeness to Kristy, the fact that I both enjoyed her and felt a commonality with her, made me gloss over differences. Maybe they were just good at their cover-up.

Kristy did not think Joe would come back any time soon. But to her surprise and my dismay he drove up an hour later while we were still sitting on the couch. He walked in the door, his face a mask of anger. He did not say anything to us. "We haven't found the keys yet," I said, trying to joke with him. "But then we haven't really been looking." No response from Joe, who was out of our sight in the kitchen, opening and closing drawers. My fears started to get the best of me.

In the past hour I had learned that Joe had served six years in prison on assault charges for trying to run over a policewoman. Kristy had kept copies of the America's Most Wanted posters of him. I also learned that he had committed countless violent burglaries. "He would tie them up and tape their mouths shut while he robbed the place," Kristy told me. Further, Kristy had described Joe's physical and verbal abuse of his ex-wife. Kristy attributes this woman's suicide to his treatment of her. More recently, he had shattered the jaw and cheekbone of another girlfriend. She is severely disfigured and is still waiting for reconstructive surgery. "I don't know what makes me different from them," Kristy told me. "But he wouldn't do that to me." I was less certain about that.

As I listened intently to Joe's movements in the kitchen, I was paralyzed by fear. I too was being controlled by his violence. I wanted to comply with him. I wanted to pacify him. I was scared. I thought about going in and trying to reason with him, but I was too fearful of what he might do. I even suggested to Kristy that we look for the keys. But she whispered back, "Let's wait and see what he does," her eyes wide and frightened. I really wanted to escape, but I could not bring myself to desert Kristy. I stood up and said, in what I hoped was a normal voice, that I was going outside to check on the children. I asked Kristy to come with me.

Joe, who had found the keys in one of the kitchen drawers, began putting his stuff in the truck. "He's packing," Kristy said to me as we walked across the street to where the children were playing with water guns in a neighbor's yard. I tried to persuade her to leave with me, even though I was worried about what Joe would do if he saw us all get in my car. She wanted me to stay longer but I refused. Ultimately, I left her there as Joe continued to carry his belongings from the house out to his truck and Kristy tried to round up the kids for dinner in an attempt at normalcy. Sadly, it was normal—or at least commonplace.

"I don't want anything you cook," JR told her, and I sadly imagined that he had been listening to Joe for too long. Kristy promised me that she would tell the upstairs neighbor, another client, to call the police if she heard anything worrisome (there was no phone in Kristy's apartment). She also promised to meet me in the morning. I went home for a sleepless night. Social workers burn out pretty fast.

The next day Kristy told me that she was ready to leave Joe.

Joe had not spent the night at the apartment, but she knew he would return eventually. I helped her and the kids move while Joe was at work. The kids were nervous and confused and asked if they could stay with me. I explained that they could not. JR said he thought everything would be okay if I were the one who found a place for them. I was torn between being flattered and depressed. I believed that the only safe place for her to go was a domestic violence shelter. Joe would find her in WCC housing or at her relatives. But she could not go straight into a shelter, because she had five days to serve in jail for a theft charge. So we vouchered her into a motel, made arrangements for the kids while she was in jail, and planned to meet after a holiday weekend to find a domestic violence program for her.

When I picked Kristy up at the motel six days later, I knew something was wrong. She had not served her time in jail; she said her child-care arrangements had fallen through. I had worried this might happen and had fought off my desire to take the kids for those few days. Of course, that would not only have crossed professional boundaries but would be grounds to terminate my employment. Also, it was a desire generated from the part of myself that wanted to "save" Kristy—to take over her life, to fix it, to make it mine. And as my director/mentor Margaret told me on numerous occasions, "We are here to serve families, not to save them." The attempt and the desire to "save" are disrespectful of clients, undermining their own competencies and autonomy by inflating our own. And Kristy's life is not mine. I have to leave it to her. But the counterpressures are sometimes powerful.

Joe, who had been calling me to find out where Kristy was and telling me that I had better not have sent her to one of those "women's places," found out her whereabouts by threatening one of her cousins. Kristy was hesitant to tell me that she and Joe had celebrated the Fourth of July together and that now she was less sure about the breakup and of what she wanted to do.

I explained to Kristy that a domestic violence shelter was the only option I could support. Our program was not safe for her if she wanted to be away from Joe. He would know where to find her. Furthermore, we could no longer serve the family if she decided to stay with Joe. WCC does not serve families where active abuse is known to be going on, because the agency refuses to support domestic violence in that way. Indeed, now that Kristy had been in contact with Joe again, even her shelter possibilities were limited. Domestic violence programs require that you keep the location of their safe houses absolutely secret, and they are very strict about clients being committed to their separations. I said I could help her go to a shelter out of town if that's what she wanted.

Kristy cried through most of the meeting. She felt betrayed and angry with me. She said she had finally told me the truth about Joe, and now I was punishing her for doing so. She did not want to leave town; she did not want to go to a domestic violence shelter and "have to hide from everyone." It was clear that she thought the limited options I gave her were forcing her back to Joe. Eventually, she refused to continue talking. She left my office and sat down at the table in the day shelter, sobbing. Her six-year-old son put his arms around her like a comforting adult. They left. A couple weeks later I heard that Joe and Kristy found a new place to live together.

It was hard to not feel angry with her, hard to not feel as though she made the wrong decision and that now her children would suffer for it as well. I think of those children with whom I spent many hours, and a voice within me flares up in anger.

Kristy is caught in a system of options that are distinctly unsatisfactory. She finds herself unable or unwilling to go toward a world of unknowns—a world that offers "safety" only in conjunction with alienation from family and friends. She wants to escape the world of threat and abuse. But the costs of escape seem awfully high. She knows that the fault will be placed entirely on her if she refuses the assistance offered. But she cannot help feeling rageful about the alternatives that are available.

After Kristy went back to Joe, I only saw her a couple of times when she stopped in to pick up mail and belongings from the office. There was clearly tension between us, and although we were polite, our closeness and rapport had evaporated. She no longer trusted me. I suppose I had taught her that you must keep the fact of abuse a secret from any caseworker if you expect to maintain assistance if and when you return to your abuser.

For a while I even worried that Joe would try to retaliate against me for encouraging Kristy to leave, and I would drive home from the office nervously checking for his truck in my rearview mirror. Her earlier reassurances—that she didn't think Joe would retaliate because he "liked me a lot"—did not comfort me much. After all, he "loved" her. I was grateful that I had not succumbed to my temptation to invite them over for that barbecue and glad my address remained unknown. It was a time of sleepless nights when I worried about Kristy and the kids, about my own safety, about my professional competence and my personal judgment. My initial opinion of Joe jeopardized my confidence in my own assessments.

Then there was silence. For a couple of months the only reminder of Kristy was the occasional piece of mail that would come for her at the office. I would return them, "Address Unknown." But three months later Kristy reappeared. I was excited and relieved to see her. We sat and talked, taking on our familiar roles of case manager/client and quasi friends, although neither category really fit anymore.

Kristy was living outside of town in a cottage on property

owned by Joe's boss. She did not have to pay rent there and the kids had room to play. She was very close to her landlords and felt secure that she could live there as long as she wanted. They "promised" her this, even though she had no lease. She and Joe had had another fight. He left for a week, staying at another girlfriend's house, she suspected. He returned and tried to kick them out of the house. But his boss refused to allow this, insisting instead that he leave, although Joe continued to work for him.

Kristy came in a couple of more times after that. The last time I saw her, Joe had not been living with her for a month. She occasionally saw him at his work site or when he came to pick up something. She "hoped" she wouldn't go back to him, but she was not ready to rule this out completely. She said the kids did not seem convinced that he was really gone for good either. JR still got terrified when he thought Joe was coming over. Kristy seemed to feel it was up to Joe whether he came back or not. She thought he might have just moved on to another girlfriend. A saddening thought, on the one hand, given his history of battering all his partners, but certainly better for Kristy.

Meanwhile, Kristy said, she was working on herself. She started exercising regularly and dieting, the latter of which I encouraged her to forget since she was so thin already. She said boredom had made her start thinking about going to a community college and pursuing a career, although she was not sure what her interests were. She returned to counseling after several months of not going and renewed her prescription for Prozac, which she had also stopped taking. She expressed interest in taking parenting classes, saying that JR had been acting out a lot. Her relationship to Joe undoubtedly caused him a lot of pain and anger.

Kristy warmed back up to me, although she maintained stronger boundaries, not telling me exactly where she was living or giving out her phone number. Maybe she knew I had called Children's Services once the abuse was disclosed (they did nothing, but that is another story). Or perhaps she just had a heightened fear of social service intervention in general. I was happy to see the children—Sue Ellen, who threw herself at me, and JR, whom I heard asking for me as he walked in the front door but who then backed away in embarrassment when he actually saw me. I hugged him anyway and sat cross-legged with him on the floor in the play area, a familiar corner where he immediately resettled himself. Kristy had cut JR's hair in a Mohawk, and with a missing front tooth and a black lead mark from sticking a pencil in his gums he looked more like a tough and hardened teenager than a six-year-old. Sue Ellen had lost her glasses and was back to bringing objects right up to her nose in order to see them. I walked them to the agency door on their way out. Kristy laughed her nervous laugh. We said goodbye.

A year later I called Kristy from my home in California where I had been writing this book. I wanted to check in with her and to see if she would be interested in reviewing this story and giving me feedback on it. Joe answered the phone. He and Kristy were living together again. Kristy told me she was in a nursing program at a community college and said she was doing well. I told Kristy about the story, but I didn't send it to her. I felt there was too much risk that Joe might read it. He would likely get angry at his portrayal and might take it out on her. Kristy agreed that maybe it would be best not to have the story around—at least not right now. She laughed in spite of herself.

Reflecting Kristy

What is there in Kristy's laugh, a laugh that punctuates this story throughout? In many ways Kristy's laughter marks the irony that helps her understand both her own life and the cultural conditions of that life. Kristy quickly rose to laughter when she reflected on the twists and turns of her life. Her life was not predictable to her either.

She laughs, for instance, at the image of herself at her grandfather's funeral in tight blue jeans and high heels, nine months pregnant and terrified by the experience of her water breaking. Her laughter betrays a sense of transgression and fatefulness that exceeds the specific words she offers. Her clothing, her lack of clear expectations about the birth, and even her attendance at a funeral scramble common images of impending motherhood. But they fit her circumstances. While she laughs at the ridiculousness of it all, she also suggests that there is more here than just an unfamiliar image of pregnancy and motherhood. She offers a glimpse of the shock, the fear, and the uncertainty that her labor and her motherhood embodied for her. Kristy's way of telling her story somehow expresses the place of irony, mishap, and strangeness in her life. Her style of being reveals the tensions between cultural norms to which she is hesitantly attached and those uncertainties of life on the edge that render them inapplicable.

Dominant paradigms tend to reduce lives like Kristy's either to the effect of structural causes or to the result of unwise decisions or some combination thereof. While both types of factors are at work, there are also many singular twists and turns involved in Kristy's homelessness. Homelessness cannot be understood or permanently resolved unless this complex web of decisions, accidents, and intrusions is taken into account. When we look into a life story for answers, for specific explanations, we overlook the interplay between the role of fortuity and the absence of structural cushions in a life like Kristy's.

An emphasis on social and/or individual responsibility also suggests a kind of inevitability. If we identify the supposed cause of Kristy's homelessness, then we imply that homelessness is a necessary outcome of that condition, when it may be that one or two different turns of decision could have moved things in another direction. I am not suggesting, of course, that institutionalized discrimination, rising costs of living, and destructive policies toward the poor simply occur by accident. Nor am I suggesting that the lives I present here are simply explained by "misfortune," in which neither responsibility nor irresponsibility plays a role. However, I am suggesting that arguments that rely on a model of either social causation or individual responsibility—or some combination thereof—subtract the role that individual circumstance and unexpected concatenations of events often play in the production of homelessness. Lives are seldom governed by simple patterns, decisions, or characteristics. They are compilations of polyvalent embodiments, relations, and circumstances that produce sometimes predictable and sometimes surprising outcomes.

Kristy does not fit stereotypes perpetuated by either political conservatives or liberals. For example, conservatives may want to point to her as lazy, irresponsible, or criminal. And liberals might want to characterize her as someone caught in cycles of poverty and abuse. Indeed, Kristy embodies elements from both of these models. That is why such reductions are so easy to make. However, the circuitous route her story follows unsettles the sufficiency of both theories. It is difficult to pinpoint a set of causal factors or a couple of acts of clear irresponsibility and say, without oversimplification, "Aha! That's why she became homeless." The story of "what went wrong" is not transparent. It is too filled with untimely accidents, innocent decisions with unexpected consequences, bad decisions with fateful implications that outstrip them, and unusual combinations—all set in a life without the backup of a stable support system. And as she shows, people do not sit tidily under the labels applied to them.

So Kristy's story illustrates the need to challenge existing frameworks that surround homeless families. Through her defiance of stereotypes and predictability, Kristy's story calls for more complex understandings of individual lives. Furthermore, her own reflections offer insight into the conditions of her life, even while her voice is silenced in larger cultural settings.

While I do not pretend to offer a complete narrative of Kristy's life, I do hope to grasp some of its complexity and surprising turns. If you sliced up her life to fit a set of analytical categories, these surprises and nuances might get lost. Her stories and reflections would simply become vehicles for fairly categorical arguments. For example, you might call on Kristy's words to illustrate a point about domestic violence or drug addiction or family dynamics. But Kristy would be dissolved into pieces and fragments. Her story would be broken into various examples without allowing the turns and surprises in it to accumulate into a specific result.

Of course, we cannot proceed without categories. We can only render them more fluid, reconfigure their complexity, and subject ourselves to tests that may expose why we are attached to one simple model of interpretation or another. Kristy's story informs the categories by which I organize the rest of this study, but it also reveals how these categories are insufficient to the people studied. The discussions I elaborate in later chapters around motherhood, violence, addiction, social service client–staff dynamics, and welfare all make up pieces of Kristy's story. They all appear somewhere in it even if they do not fully constitute it. In what follows I try to both uncover some of the patterns that shape the lives of these women and to remain attentive to those differential accumulations of little events that so often play a distinctive role in engendering and circumscribing homeless mothers.

2. Motherly Things

Mythical Mothers: The Susan Smith Case

Dichotomies of the moralized poles of the good virtuous mother and the evil neglectful one are carefully maintained in the public imagination and in public policies (Tsing 1990; Fineman and Karpin 1995; Roberts 1991; Mink 1995; Ladd-Taylor and Umansky 1998). For example, consider a case that helped to solidify and illustrate this dichotomy—the Susan Smith case. This case took place in 1994 when a white South Carolina woman claimed that a Black man carjacked her and abducted her two young sons. She was later found guilty of their murders, having pushed her car into a lake. The children both drowned.

The Susan Smith case holds a special fascination for me because it sparks one of those debates where the crevice between liberals and conservatives deepens and where many from both sides fall into the canyon together, making a host of unlikely companions. When analyzing the media reactions to this case, one cannot fail to note the public horror toward the image of two children victimized by the same person expected to devote and sacrifice her life for them. How could anyone be so heartless, cruel, selfish, and calculating? Or alternatively, if somewhat less common, how could someone be so unstable and pathological without being detected until after the tragedy occurred?

My goal is not to attempt an explanation of Susan Smith's behavior, nor to contribute to the cultural preoccupation with her punishment. What I am doing is to ponder the role that conceptions of motherhood play in portraying Susan Smith either as a monster or as a victim of mental instability. My work with homeless mothers has led me to consider how motherhood is associated with a complex set of traits that are represented as universal (nurturing, sacrifice, nonviolence). The "naturalness" of motherhood makes any deviation from that identity uniquely abhorrent (Scheper-Hughes 1992).

Susan Smith was tried not simply as a murderer but as a white mother who killed. Middle- and upper-class white women in the United States are bound more closely to the cult of perfect mothering, while Black women are more readily assumed to be deviant mothers and their children viewed as less socially valuable (Roberts 1995; Solinger 1992). Thus, the transgression of motherhood norms by white women is a particularly rich metaphor for understanding how race politics contribute to the cultural fascination with "bad" mothers (Ladd-Taylor and Umansky 1998; Mink 1995). Mothers who are bad or deemed to be "monsters" (Tsing 1990) or "Other" (Polakow 1993) legitimate social enforcement of good-mother codes of conduct by offering an allegedly dangerous anti-model. This process of normalization negates the continuum of behavior that more adequately represents how women live their lives. In effect, the model of normal motherhood is produced and enforced even though it does not adequately represent the experiences of mothers—even those purported to embody the ideal. Thus, a fiction is generated that is potentially destructive to all mothers and children. Furthermore, the model of the normal mother creates a series of intense difficulties and binds for homeless mothers living in circumstances far removed from those implicitly assumed to surround normal mothers.

When Susan Smith was at the center of public attention and hostility, she became an icon of antimaternity. And through her representation of all that good motherhood is not, she thereby reinforced an idealized version of good motherhood. The romanticization of the "good mother" is so pervasive that it impacts women in all social strata—for example, women who work and leave their children in the care of others; or women who cannot afford or find adequate housing for their children; or women whose lives are so full of pain, violence, sickness, and/or poverty that their children are not at its center.

Consider how the cultural staging of normal motherhood might affect someone like Sally, a thirty-three-year-old white woman and client at Westside Community Center (WCC).

"I wanted kids . . . but [then again] I didn't," said Sally, looking over at me from her cramped kitchen table. Behind her there was an American flag on the wall. "But my perfect ideal life was I wanted to be married and have kids." Sally has never been married. She has three boys from three different fathers. The first father ran a nude modeling agency that employed her; the second never knew she was pregnant; and the last one is now in prison:

> He stabbed some guy several times in the chest and it took the other guy's life. If the guy hadn't have died, then he wouldn't have got so severe [a sentence]. . . . Me and him, we will eventually be married. . . . I've moved with my kids . . . to protect my kids, even though it might look bad on their school

records. . . . I did it to protect my kids 'cause if I'd stayed, my kids woulda kept getting abused or myself, and I was always in fear.

At one time I had to give my kids up temporarily because I was afraid I was gonna hurt them. I was really close to my first breakdown. I had such a breakdown I couldn't even remember if I had kids or not. . . . Like I said, it's been extremely hectic, really spastic sometimes, being a single parent for what I've gone through. . . . My life or death don't mean nothing to me. . . . I would give my life, whatever, in a heartbeat for my kids. No problem.

The distance between "I wanted kids but I didn't" and "I would give my life in a heartbeat for my kids" reflects an ambivalence that haunts Sally and, as I have discovered, many homeless mothers. Sally expresses other motherly ambivalences and contradictions:

Me and my kids have been through so much. And I know they love me with all their heart. And I love them. But . . . I just wish I didn't have the part—what they consider abuse. I'm working on it at least. I'm so afraid of losing my kids and I don't want to lose my kids. They would have to kill me to take my kids, whether I accidentally hurt them or not. . . . I don't care if it's the law or not, nobody will get my kids after what I've encountered and had to go through. That's the one thing I can say is mine. The good Lord gave them to me, and He's the only one that's gonna take them from me. I feel like that with all my heart. 'Cause like I said, at least I did have my kids when we went through what we did. At least I have something that I can say that's part of me, you know?

Sally is defensive about her parenting, warning that even if she hurts her kids "accidentally," she still will not consent to their removal. To Sally, to hurt her children accidentally is to hurt them without explicitly or consciously meaning to. Her language is testimony to the ways in which she feels out of control in her parenting, even while feeling protective of her right to parent. Sally stresses her love for her children but also her need for them as witnesses and for companionship through tumultuous life events. Yet Sally's children have not just endured tribulations with her; they are part of what she has endured, and therefore, "nobody will get my kids after what I've encountered and had to go through."

Even though Sally's own lived experiences of parenting are at odds with the larger cultural model of the good mother—that is, a woman who is devoted to and sacrifices for her children—she nonetheless subscribes to this model. Yet it is this model that presses women to erase any ambivalence accompanying their efforts to raise their children under difficult conditions. Sally's self-presentation clearly maintains the tensions between the good mother model drawn from the larger culture and the actual circumstances of her mothering.

One route to thinking about cultural models of motherhood is to explore sites where such norms are produced and enforced. Social service settings are just such arenas. Indeed, social services have taken on the role of regulating mothers for a long time (Ladd-Taylor and Umansky 1998; Appell 1998; Gordon 1994; Skocpol 1992; Mink 1995). As Linda Gordon points out, in the early 1900s the kind of intervention promoted to help poor single mothers changed. Previously, the emphasis had been on providing charity and moral reform. However, in the early 1900s single motherhood was recast as a more pressing social problem, and social service agencies were employed to not only provide relief for the impoverished but to bring diverse parenting practices into conformity with middle-class norms of the time (Gordon 1994; Mink 1995).

These paradigms continue to resonate through social service programs today. Indeed, at WCC staff members take seriously the position of evaluating families and breaking patterns of violence, abuse, and neglect. While such issues are not limited to low-income people, their lives are so often entwined with social service systems that such labels get attached to them easily (Roberts 1991, 1434). Thus, part of the project of serving families becomes teaching and enforcing particular familial codes to clients. For example, WCC has a "no-hitting" policy, which means that while you are in the program you are not allowed to discipline your children harshly. (Subsumed under this policy is a dictate against all other forms of harsh punishment, including yelling.) The staff see clients' time in the program as an "opportunity" for them to learn nonabusive disciplinary techniques. As is the case with rules in general, this one is enforced to different degrees depending on the individual client and caseworker.

The program director, Margaret, explains the policy, saying that staff should not be in the position of distinguishing between "appropriate" spanking and child abuse. Therefore, they must insist that no physical punishment be used in order to avoid confusion. While the no-hitting policy is designed to protect children, it also functions to protect staff. As Margaret admitted to me one day, she just does not want to be around such dynamics. Furthermore, staff do not want to be held accountable by other staff or external agencies for not addressing neglectful or abusive behaviors.

The no-hitting and no-yelling mandates are challenging for many clients to adhere to—if not impossible for some. They are thrust into new environments (here I refer particularly to the day and night shelters where these rules are the easiest to enforce), and they are surrounded by other families and staff, all of whom are potentially watching their behavior. Since children tend to experience high levels of stress in shelters, it often produces disciplinary issues in an environment where many of the tools that they have relied on to control their children are deemed inappropriate and potentially abusive. Clients also know, partly from street knowledge but also from the many forms they must sign when they come into the program, that WCC staff are "mandatory reporters." This means that staff members are obligated to report any signs or incidences of child abuse to the Children's Services Division, a federal agency that has a reputation of acting inconsistently and sometimes arbitrarily (Appell 1998).

Many clients complained about the no-hitting and no-yelling policy. They said they needed to yell at or spank their children in order to get them to mind. Many implied, and others outright asserted, that since I do not have children, I do not understand the nature of discipline. Michelle, a white twenty-year-old pregnant mother of one, looked me straight in the eye after I asked her to lower her voice with her daughter in the day shelter, saying, "Debbie, sometimes you *have* to yell at your kids or spank them. Otherwise, they don't hear you."

While I am sometimes uncomfortable, frustrated, and even indignant when I witness parents being particularly harsh with their children, it is worth considering the ways in which agency policies dictate norms of motherhood. Implicit in the no-hitting policy are certain standards that automatically place mothers at WCC under a cloud of suspicion. The very existence of the rule suggests to clients, staff, and outsiders a "problem" in parenting, a need for regulation and control. It also makes mothers feel that they are being parented themselves.

In a session with a client in which we were discussing discipline, I asked this mom if she ever hit her child.

"I don't abuse him, if that's what you mean," she replied, bristling with obvious defensiveness. "I've spanked him before, but I don't *beat* him!" She kept her eyes turned away from me as she said this, the anger in her voice apparent. What this client understood, and took offense at, was that my questioning of her disciplinary practices called into question the very nature of her role as a mother. My query implied to her that I viewed her as a person who was in fact capable of abuse and furthermore that I might expose her as such, thereby placing her under additional control.

The mothers I worked with at WCC resented any implication that their "proper" maternity was being called into question. However, simultaneously they had complex and sometimes paradoxical relationships to their children, to their identities as mothers, and to outside representations of motherhood. For example, without any prompting from me, Sally said this about the Susan Smith case, which was receiving heavy media attention at the time of our interviews:

> And then you hear this thing, this lady finally admitted to killing those two boys. And I'm sitting there, man, I just started crying this morning when I heard that. I said, "Man, I hope they throw the book at you, lady." But yet, I shouldn't feel that, because maybe there was . . . maybe she's got . . . you know? I try to think of other people, too, but it's just, something I just cannot see, you know? And because especially where I've hurt my kids sometimes. Where there's been a couple times where I've lost control with the kids. But I turned myself in and they worked with me.

Sally is horrified by the crime and feels Smith should be punished severely. In this way Sally distances herself from Smith. Smith lost control completely, committing the ultimate sin. While Sally can look down on Smith with a punitive gaze, she also struggles with her identifications with Smith. She suggests, not quite finishing her sentences, that "maybe there was [a reason], maybe she's got [a reason]." Sally knows that for her mothering is a struggle, and she wants that aspect of mothering to be more widely acknowledged. One can imagine that she stutters because she does not want to convey the impression that it is acceptable to let her violent impulses win out, yet she simultaneously recognizes that those impulses do exist:

> I hope and pray to God that I never lose my temper again. And before I feel like I'm gonna do that again, and I hate to say this, I'll get something where I can calm myself complete-ly down. . . . That's part of the reason why I got on a lot of downer drugs, so that way I wouldn't lose it. Because there's been a lot of times when I've thought, "God, I'm gonna kill my kids." That's a horrible thought! It's horrible! But the only way I would not get that out is to pop some downers, drink a bottle of Jack, no problem. I drink that stuff like Kool-Aid. I could drink a couple of fifths or pints in a day. . . . My kids, they think, "Oh wow, mommy, she's not mad." They didn't realize a lot of times it's because I was in my own little world on drugs. . . . But I still managed to do a lot of the motherly things. . . . I didn't know how else to do it. . . . Because a lot of times I just feel like I'm going to lose control completely. I hate feeling that way because I feel helpless when I feel that way.

Sally's relationship to her children is an ambivalent one, a combination of love, resentment, and the sense of being overwhelmed. She also struggles with a terrifying acknowl-edgment that she is not always in control of herself. She uses desperate strategies to protect her children from her—strategies that deviate from mainstream standards of positive parenting and that place her own life and the custody of her children in further jeopardy. But, she argues, these strategies keep her children relatively safe.

Sally claims to use drugs and alcohol to diffuse her anger. "I hate to say this," she says and then confesses that she would use drugs and alcohol again if she felt as though she needed to protect her kids from herself. Of course, one should be wary of an addict's claim that drugs and alcohol help her maintain positive parenting. While drug and alcohol use might at times calm a person down, such behaviors are just as likely, if not more so, to promote violence and a sense of being out of control. Further, Sally's own version of why she uses them could provide an excuse for future use.

It may be that drugs and alcohol provide at least a temporary numbing against the hatred inside of Sally, hatred that was instilled in her during her own upbringing and that continues to wreak havoc on her life and the lives of her children. Yet these kinds of negotiations between anger, violence, and drug use are precisely what is erased from idealized versions of motherhood. Mythical mothers do not experience rage at their children; they never lose control; they do not use drugs (at least not illicit ones) to keep themselves from lashing out at their families. The erasure of these paradoxes and negotiations from discourses on the normal family pushes to the margin those unable to fulfill the ideal even superficially.[1] It also intensifies support for regulatory and penal systems as the only solutions, leaving mothers like Sally with bleak options.

> I know what I'm capable of doing in a really bad time, and that part scares me. I hate myself for that part, but [also] that's the part I hate my stepparents for. I will probably go to hell for the hate I have. And I hope it doesn't end up killing me, because I'm not a hateful person really. . . . But the hate, it just gets to me so bad. . . . I mean, that's just how I survive—by lying, stealing, doing drugs. I've done jobs that most women wouldn't even think of doing in their lives—just to survive.

Earlier, when Sally talked about "turning herself in," she was referring to an incident when she had beaten all of her boys bloody with a switch and then had turned herself in to the Children's Services Division. At that time, a time she describes as a nervous breakdown, she gave up her children to foster care while she tried to address her mental health issues. Perhaps it is this kind of personal experience that prompts Sally to both relate to and distinguish herself from Smith. Unlike Smith, Sally was able to acknowledge that her behavior was dangerous, even life threatening, and she took steps to contain it. Smith did not—perhaps could not.

The Smith murders, as well as other forms of child abuse or endangerment, are intolerable. However, one of the questions that its media coverage poses is how good motherhood is constructed antithetically to "monster mothers" (Tsing 1990). Susan Smith did not just commit the social crime of murder. Susan Smith revealed, to quote *Newsweek,* just "how much evil can lurk in even a mother's heart" (1995, 28). The heart, according to *Newsweek*'s imagery, is the place where maternal love is supposed to reside. It is the embodiment of care and nurturance. Yet Susan Smith's heart is instead tainted with "evil"—an evil so dark that it can lurk in even a mother's heart.

While one could view this statement through the simple lens of media exploitation, I believe it reveals a great deal more about cultural norms. These representations of antimothers, monster mothers, and Other mothers can be understood as one facet of a cultural drive to monitor mothers, regulate them intensively, and steer them toward fictive models of normality. The population most affected by such regulatory trends is women who are already marginalized—those who are already suspect because their poverty, their lack of education, and their immersion in pain render them unable to act out the middle-class ideal.

Homeless mothers must either struggle to achieve impossible norms or risk being placed into the dependent category of the incompetent mother. The good mother and her antithesis are produced together through powerful cultural discourses. Such productions protect the impossible model of the good mother by translating homeless mothers into cultural scapegoats. In this way, poor white mothers join the ranks of poor women of color and lesbian mothers, social categories that are deemed outside of normal motherhood. When you see how these two myths intersect and determine each other, then you see the need to change both.

Mothering Daughters

What does it feel like to grow up in a family that is vastly different from idealized portrayals of family life? Most of us have this experience to some degree. For some, that experience is more dramatic. This perceived discrepancy tends to be heightened by the fact that a chaotic and abusive childhood is primarily acknowledged through a cultural ethos that fixes all the blame on particular family members. Such individualized blaming increases the pressures on already burdened identities.

Terry, a nineteen-year-old mixed-race woman (of Dutch and Native American heritage) can remember little about her life before the age of ten. She has a few flitting memories. She remembers opening a can of beer for her dad, covering him with a blanket on the couch; she recalls being sexually abused by her brother; she remembers smoking cigarettes and pot at the age of eight. Here is one of her early memories:

> I woke up one night to my mom screaming bloody murder,
> just screaming. . . . I opened my door and my dad has this
> shotgun, he was trying to kill her. I was just going, "What in
> the hell?" and I hid in my room. I wasn't coming out. . . .
> I don't remember what happened. I just remember we were
> in the car and we were running. And my mom's telling me if
> my dad finds us he's gonna rape me and he's gonna kill my
> brother and he's gonna kill her. . . . A week ago my dad was
> perfect and now he's this horrible man that's gonna kill us

and rape me. . . . We ran. . . . He wasn't supposed to know where we were, it was this big hiding secret. Then my mom went back to him and everything was "great" again.

Terry was ten at the time. In retrospect at least, Terry recognizes that things were not actually great when they returned. The smooth surface of the family was always a cover for more troubled dynamics stirring underneath. These dynamics, one may speculate, could account for Terry's memory lapses.

What Terry remembers about her later childhood is characterized by depression, several suicide attempts, drug and alcohol abuse, and an active sexual life in her pre- and early teen years. She was bounced back and forth between her parents after they separated and her mother moved across the country with a new husband. Terry's mother had frequent bouts of depression while Terry lived with her. Terry describes what family life was like when she was twelve:

> I felt like I had to be there for them [her mother and step-father] because my mom, she went through like six nervous breakdowns and she wouldn't talk to men, she would only talk to me. So I had to be strong, and I wasn't able to tell them about my pain. You know, my mom would just be . . . locked in the bathroom, rocking herself. I was the only one that [she would] let in, and I would rock her and I would hold her. "It's okay, Mom, it's okay, it's okay, Mom, we'll make it through, we'll make it through it." And she would try to kill herself, and I would dig the medicine out of her mouth and say, "No, you're gonna live." . . . I had to be the psychiatrist there. I had to be the strong one. I couldn't tell them about my pain. . . . So I didn't want to die, but I couldn't handle that. I just kind of wanted to go away for a while so that I could get a break and start fresh. . . . So I overdosed. . . . I kept saying, "Just let me go to hell, just let me go to hell."

Terry portrays herself as a strong and capable woman, capable of saving her mother. But she also acknowledges that these family dynamics overwhelmed her, that her own pain and confusion were at times too much for her to take. In her attempts to mother her mother, a role that she says had to be adopted because of her gender (her mother "wouldn't talk to men"), Terry sacrificed her own needs and well-being. She is the good mother—sacrificial and devoted. While Terry expresses a certain pride in her strength, it does not make her feel worthy. Recall that she imagines herself descending to "hell."

After her suicide attempt, Terry moved back across the country to her California hometown to live with her father and brother. She says her dad was rarely around—he was "constantly partying." And she describes her own thirteen-year-old life as a "big party." She was not attending school, was using alcohol and drugs extensively, and was indiscriminately sexually active:

> I had had a problem with sexual promiscuity. I was either always having sex with someone or I was being sexually abused, constantly. . . . You name it—people at stores, people I was dating, people I had never met, people walking down the street trying to drag me into a car—you just name it and it was happening. That was my life, sex was my whole life. . . . [Then] I said, "I can't do this no more," and I gave myself a promise. I said, "All right, I'm not gonna have sex with anybody anymore, not unless I decide to be in a relationship." And I did.

Terry's out-of-control sexual behavior might not be surprising. Recall her earliest memories. Her father threatens to murder the others, but Terry he will rape. So from an early age Terry understands herself as a potentially sexualized victim. Terry also identified herself as a victim of early sexual abuse by her older brother.

Shortly after she decided to abstain from sex until she was in a committed relationship, she met seventeen-year-old Carlos:

> I kind of took him under my wing, and I saw him as something I could shape and something I could take care of, you know? I saw him as like my little child. . . . I always had this need to take care of something, you know? If it wasn't a cat, it was an adult, and I took care of my dad very well, too. I was my dad's mom basically, too. Well, I was the mother of everybody . . . but this person especially I could mother him, and I liked that. It made me feel needed and it made me feel wanted.

Terry feels the weight of responsibility to care for those around her, including those much older and those who would traditionally care for her. Her parents, her brother, her boyfriend, even stray cats are seen as her responsibility. Like many children who grow up with alcoholic or drug-addicted parents, she is the surrogate mother figure.

Terry's story offers a glimpse into the ways in which young girls and women from an early age mimic the traditional mothering roles that women are expected to embody (Chodorow 1978). Terry's desire to feel and act indispensable to her mother, to protect her father, and to be needed and wanted by her boyfriend is presented through the rubric of maternity. Yet Terry's embodiment of maternal expression unsettles the very core of motherhood ideals. Her relationships are influenced by cultural ideals but are set in conditions that are radically at odds with them.

For other homeless women, mothering their daughters challenges their abilities to adhere to cultural models of mother love. Consider Hannah, a twenty-five-year-old white woman and mother of three, discussing her relationship with her five-year-old daughter Amber:

After I had her, it's like Joe [Amber's father] took care of her. I just wouldn't go near her or nothing. . . . I guess 'cause he was paying a lot of attention to her, and he pushed me and Bobby [her oldest son of a different father] to the back burner after she was born, 'cause it was his first daughter and all. . . . I still get mad about it. . . . I guess more, I'd say, jealous because she gets a lot of attention from him and he pushes everyone else aside. So I just get frustrated, not knowing what to do. So I kind of like push her aside every once in a while. I mean I didn't want to, but I've caught myself even saying I hated her. I love her to a point but. . . . It's not like I *hate her* hate her, but I guess it's just frustrating not knowing where you stand.

Hannah acknowledges that Amber has heard her say that she hates her. She says her daughter reminds her of her own little sister, of whom she was always jealous. So Hannah ends up trying to get back at her sister by rejecting her daughter, as well as displacing her own feelings of rejection from her husband onto her daughter.

Hannah's behavior does not fit the ideal of mother love. On the contrary, she exposes the ambivalent emotions of a mother struggling to raise a child whose place in her life is highly ambiguous. Hannah clearly has concerns about her relationship to her daughter ("I don't *hate her* hate her"), but she acknowledges only loving Amber "to a point." Hannah's relationship to her daughter has to do with her own experiences as a child as well as the gendered competition for her husband. These are not dynamics traditionally accepted or acknowledged in cultural characterizations of mother love. Yet Hannah is aware of the social norms of mother love. She believes that jealousy, resentment, and ambivalence are not acceptable reasons to reject a child. And so she later provides a more socially acceptable gloss on her relationship with Amber:

"I guess I expect too much from her. . . . I want her to have a better life than I did. I guess I'm harder on her for that."

Hannah's ambivalence engenders uncertain sentiments in me. On the one hand, I feel myself wanting to protect Amber. I see her in my mind's eye, building a highway out of blocks with her younger brother on the floor of the day shelter, her hand reaching up to push her overgrown blond bangs out of her eyes every few minutes, as they pursue the project. I wonder what it might mean for her to grow up with a mom whose complicated feelings for her are more aligned with hate, disdain, and jealousy than with unconditional motherly love. The unfairness of it unsettles me. But I am also aware that ambivalences usually accompany all expressions of mothering, even in the most favorable circumstances. Maternal love does not magically begin at conception, at birth, or at any fixed moment. Mothers relate to their children and to the perplexities of parenting in diverse ways, even though most are haunted by a univocal model of mothering. The production of multiple models adjusted to different contexts could serve both Hannah and her daughter. It might alleviate the immense pressure on their relationship; it might produce several possibilities and places for nurturance and love.

Feminist ethnographers have explored conceptions and practices of mothering in a variety of contexts (Glenn et al. 1994; Harris 1997; Polakow 1993; Ragoné 1994; Luker 1996; Kaplan 1997; Scheper-Hughes 1992). And many feminist theorists have sought to revalue the traditional characteristics and sentiments associated with mothering (nurturance, care, peace, love) either as innate to women or as cultural predispositions to be cultivated and praised (Chodorow 1978; Ruddick 1989). Whereas the masculine ideal in U.S. culture glorifies mothering practices while striving to render their bearers subordinate, some feminists have provided a counterdiscourse that revels in the importance and beauty of motherhood—giving it respect while trying to unbind it from subordination (Forcey 1994). The paradox of such a counterdiscourse, however, is that it is extremely difficult to lift out of the framework it resists (Tsing 1990). The glorification of "mothering traits" threatens to reinscribe the equation of maternity as womanhood with the same force that those who marginalize the practices of mothering do. It both silences and endangers women whose lives are not defined by maternal sentiment or who live in circumstances where its expression is dangerous, exploitative, or undesired.

In her research on parenting practices in an impoverished community in northeastern Brazil, Nancy Scheper-Hughes tries to break out of this discourse/counterdiscourse circle. Her work denaturalizes mother love by interpreting women's "neglect" of their children to be a consequence of larger cultural and socioeconomic constraints. Thus her analysis reframes interpretations that blame mothers, instead recognizing their disturbing behavior to reflect rational decision making under conditions of extreme poverty:

> Contemporary theories of maternal sentiment—of mother love as we know and understand it—are the product of a very specific historical context. The invention of mother love corresponds not only with the rise of the modern bourgeois nuclear family (as Elizabeth Badinter [1980] pointed out) but also with the demographic transition: the precipitous decline in infant mortality and female fertility. My argument is a materialist one: mother love as defined in the psychological, social-historical, and sociological literatures is far from universal or innate and represents instead an ideological, symbolic representation grounded in the basic material conditions that define women's reproductive lives. (Scheper-Hughes 1992, 401)

Scheper-Hughes de-essentializes mother love by arguing that parental practices and affections occur in specific economic and cultural contexts. This allows the consideration of diverse responses to parenthood as something more complex than an expression of individual pathology. Once mother love is taken out of the realm of the natural, we can examine how the ideal of good motherhood is itself culturally produced. And we can shift away from those entrenched dichotomies of good and evil that discipline so many mothers in difficult circumstances.

Sally's volatile temper, Terry's mother's need to be saved by her daughter, and Hannah's ambivalence toward her daughter are too easily incorporated into a single story of motherhood gone awry (Polakow 1993; Ladd-Taylor and Umansky 1998). This serves to reinforce a one-dimensional model of motherhood, and to treat deviations as individual failures. Such a perspective directs our attention away from understanding the social and historical circumstances and from diversifying our models. It encourages us to ask "What went wrong?" within a particular family or with an individual woman rather than try to understand the race, class, and gender dynamics in these scenarios.

To hold individuals solely responsible for their actions omits the wider social milieu. However, it remains politically unpopular to look at mothering through this lens. If we continue to locate the blame, the problem, the deviance, and the pathology solely within the individual, then we must conclude that only the individual needs fixing or, more accurately, punishing. But if we begin to view this problem from a larger social, cultural, and historical perspective, the issue appears more complex, more diffuse, and more costly to repair. Unfortunately, although we would like to deny it, the fact is that Susan Smith, Sally, Terry, and Hannah are not unique. Their behavior suggests certain patterns that, rather than creating public hysteria and backlash that seeks to stig-matize and regulate women, could instead result in social and community measures that would support and protect families.

Beyond Conception

If ambivalence and complexity often accompany mothering practices, they also participate in the stories women tell about their pregnancies. Unplanned pregnancy, and sometimes even the ones women think they plan for, can produce anxi-ety, fear, frustration, confusion, and resentment.

Consider Terry, who earlier in this essay became involved with Carlos when she was fifteen. Terry's menstrual period had always been irregular, which she attributes to her drug use (cocaine, marijuana, methamphetamines, LSD, and alco-hol). She never used birth control, because her period was so infrequent. Terry got a pregnancy test when she was two and half months pregnant and was "already showing." Terry and Carlos went to an "impersonal clinic," and there she tested positive for pregnancy: "I tell Carlos I'm pregnant in the doc-tor's office, and he picks me up and twirls me around with a big ole smile. He says, 'We're gonna do it Terry!'" At least ini-tially, Carlos found a thrill in the prospect of a child. On the other hand, Terry was worried and overwhelmed by the news of this unplanned pregnancy and felt a kind of disbelief at Carlos's enthusiasm: "And I'm going, 'Oh my God, you're crazy, you're crazy! I'm fifteen years old. I just turned fifteen! You're crazy!' You know, I probably got pregnant on my birth-day. I'm doing all these drugs. That's where I panicked—[it] was the drugs."

Another client, Michelle, a white twenty-year-old woman, described telling her then sixteen-year-old boyfriend, Tony, that she was pregnant:

Tony goes, "I'm gonna be a daddy" and he was like, all excited.
And I was like, "Oh my God." I was bawling. I mean I was really unhappy that I was pregnant. And he was like, "Michelle,
we're gonna be parents." And I'm like, "Whatever!"

The contrasting reactions between these two teenage girls
and their partners to the news of unplanned pregnancies are
revealing. Michelle's and Terry's fears are based on a premo-
nition of the responsibilities that they now face. Their lives
have been permanently altered. Male partners do not neces-
sarily face a new, permanent responsibility in their lives once
a pregnancy occurs.[2] Individual men cannot be held entirely
responsible for their lack of provision for families in the face
of systems that set up poor families for failure and that deter
the existence of two-parent families (Bourgois 1995; Gordon
1994). Still, there is an irony in Carlos's "big ole smile" when
one considers his behavior shortly after their son, Braley,
was born: "I would be breastfeeding Braley, and he [Carlos]
would throw plates and everything at me. And I would have
to shelter Braley. I would be turning on my side like this, and
my whole side would be bruised from stuff." Carlos's enthusiasm toward the idea of fatherhood did not translate into an
ability to nurture his family (see Bourgois 1995). Instead, the
added responsibility may have increased his tendency toward
violence, and Terry's increased dependency heightened her
vulnerability to being his victim.

Both Terry and Michelle expressed hesitations about their
pregnancies. Both women were uncertain about whether or
not they wanted to be parents at this point in their lives. However, both considered adoption more seriously than they
considered abortion, which is indicative of a national trend
(Luker 1996). While abortion is the more common decision
for middle-class white women, it tends to feel less acceptable
and less accessible for many poor women. As Kristin Luker

points out, abortion tends to be the choice of women who believe that they will have other opportunities available to them in the future if they postpone childbearing, such as a good education, a solid marriage, and/or a career (1996). Women estranged from those middle-class aspirations may feel less compelled to choose abortion. Instead, for some, childbearing offers something that they *can* do with their lives, and it offers the possibility of love and hope that is absent in other aspects of their lives (Kaplan 1997; Ladner 1971; Luker 1996). Furthermore, as I will discuss in more detail later, the antiabortion movement has had a profound impact on many impoverished women, framing abortion as a selfish and barbaric decision.

Adoption, on the other hand, may be experienced at least initially as something women can do for their children. Adoption is wrapped in maternal ideologies of giving— giving a good home to the child and giving a good couple a child they desire.[3] This may allow women to maintain a self-image more aligned with good motherhood ideals than abortion does. Yet adoption, while often considered by women facing unplanned pregnancies, is less often actualized as a choice than it used to be.[4] For example, Michelle describes her considerations of adoption:

> Yeah, I was gonna give her up for adoption. That went through my mind a lot. And I brought it to Tony's attention, and he got kind of hurt and upset, 'cause he wanted Marissa [their now three-year-old daughter]. I mean . . . if I woulda said, "Tony, I want to get pregnant," he probably would have said, "No way." But because I was pregnant, you know, he's like, "I want to be a dad, you know, that's pretty cool. We're gonna have a baby." He was real excited. And I hit like five months and reality hit me in the face that I was pregnant and really gonna have a baby. I felt Marissa move and I was like,

"Oh, my baby's moving," and I got to like it, and I couldn't wait to see it. . . . And I was really excited then. And it got closer and closer and I got more excited, and she was born and I was really happy.

Jane, a white twenty-seven-year-old client, also thought about putting her second child up for adoption:

Adoption came through my mind. I was scared, you know. He [her boyfriend] was still using off and on, and I had fallen down some stairs and hurt myself. And I was without a job, and I was scared. I didn't think that I could give the better home. And then I started thinking, well, what if they couldn't give her the better home? It doesn't mean they're better people—it means they have more money. Doesn't mean they'd love her more. And I can have more money, and I know that I could love her. So I made the right choice.

As Jane points out, the social pressure to give up a child for adoption is often bound to cultural ideals about what makes a good home and who makes good parents. While Jane initially feels as if she should relinquish her child since she does not meet those ideals, she eventually moves toward challenging them, calling into question the equation that greater affluence equals greater love and a better life.

As Solinger has chronicled, just a few decades ago young unmarried white women were coerced into relinquishing their children and giving them up for adoption (1992). During that era, pregnancy for women out of wedlock became pathologized, and women were under immense social pressure to give their babies up to "normal" and "healthy" two-parent middle-class couples. Unmarried Black women, on the other hand, were much more likely to keep their children, as they were alienated from the adoption market because of the lack of parents interested or willing to adopt Black infants

(Solinger 1992). And some have suggested that Black communities were by and large more willing to support and accommodate young mothers and infants in a way that middle-class white communities were not (Solinger 1992; Stack 1974). More recent studies, however, suggest that while this may have been true several decades ago, the notion that Black communities provide social support for single mothers is no longer the case (Kaplan 1997). Furthermore, the myth that Black communities implicitly support single motherhood as a choice has served to further pathologize those communities as integrally deviant and as antithetical to mainstream ideologies about the family (Kaplan 1997).

One factor that may contribute to the decisions of women of color to keep their babies is their long history of having children taken away from them by state intervention (Dorris 1989; Roberts 1991; Gordon 1994). The relationship between child welfare workers and marginalized mothers remains tense today partly for this reason. Marginalized women (e.g., poor women, women of color, disabled women, and lesbians) sometimes fear forced sterilization, a fear not unfounded given past practices with vestiges today.[5] Such histories may promote more community tolerance for "nontraditional" child bearing as well as contribute to women making the decision to bear and raise children outside of the "traditional" nuclear family (Solinger 1992).

The stigma of maternal incompetence experienced by marginalized women may prompt some of them to want to prove their social worth as good mothers. In some cases, pending motherhood may be a prod for women to reorganize their lives and try to conform more closely to middle-class standards of stability. As Terry explains:

> I was planning on adoption much stronger than abortion.
> I had paperwork and everything. And I couldn't do it. . . . I

became determined that I was going to straighten out my life and I was going to raise this baby. And I was going to give this baby everything that anybody else could. And I was prepared to do it alone at this point. . . . I wanted to give this baby a good life, a clean start.

The cultural contradictions experienced by Terry, Michelle, and Jane perhaps exemplify a cultural transition. First, they experience the cultural ideology that says that one should give one's baby to a more stable, "traditional" family. But then they find the cultural window that has been tentatively opened in more recent times, which suggests that birth mothers love their children uniquely and should raise them no matter what.

Actually, both the logic that glorifies biological motherhood and that which enforces adoption in particular circumstances are weighted with pressures and discriminations. Neither logic helps women make decisions that address the complexities of their own lives. Women are either defined as unfit based on various cultural criteria and pressed to release babies in order to adhere to social norms, or they are revered as birth mothers and pressed into a paradigm of mothering that speaks poorly to their actual circumstances.

After abortion was legalized in 1973, the social terrain in which illegitimate pregnancies occurred changed drastically. Fewer women chose adoption as a way of handling an unplanned pregnancy. And yet abortion was rarely discussed by my clients as an option that they entertained seriously. It may be that abortion is more widely considered prior to giving birth, even if it is not openly discussed after birth (Luker 1996). Perhaps once you've had the child, having contemplated abortion is uncomfortable to admit. Even to mention it as an option you considered before giving birth may suggest ambivalence about your child now.

Among clients at WCC there is a marked pro-life sentiment.

Perhaps in some cases they react to their marginal social positions by asserting their right to have and raise children. This may be even more pronounced given their histories of denial of this right. Indeed, for some, abortion may feel more like a social pressure than a freedom to choose. For example, consider the welfare reform measure in some states that dictates that benefits no longer be increased for families if a new child is born while the parent is already receiving aid (Piven 1996). This policy is allegedly meant to deter those "baby factory" recipients, who, the story goes, bear numerous children to gain the few extra dollars a month allotted for new family members. Thus, some women feel pressured into abortion either because they do not have adequate financial means to parent or because of social anger that continues to burgeon against welfare recipients who become pregnant "irresponsibly."

Given these social pressures, the language of choice embraced by proponents of abortion rights may be more problematic and inadequate for homeless women than it first appears. As Solinger notes, the idea of childbearing as a personal choice emphasizes the individual while de-emphasizing the social, political, and economic contexts in which that individual is set (1998). One is assumed to be choosing freely, unconstrained, and thus simultaneously is fully responsible for the outcomes of one's choice. So what may be missed in feminist preoccupations with protecting women's right to choose is the inextricable link between choice and consequence (Luker 1996). Women who choose to bear children under difficult conditions can then be berated as having made the "wrong choice," while the circumstances in which they had to choose continue to be unacknowledged (Solinger 1998).

As Luker notes, ideologies of choice tend to support cultural conceptions of individual blame (1996). Young mothers who are poor, uneducated, and struggling to stay above water are treated as if they chose those conditions. Luker suggests that contemporary public rhetoric blames young mothers for their own poverty, advising that these women would not be poor if they had merely postponed childbearing as their affluent counterparts are doing. She then, however, demonstrates that most of the women so characterized were already poor when they became pregnant. Their poverty is not a result of ill-reasoned choices but of a host of socioeconomic conditions that serve to promote both early childbearing and the difficulties that follow from it (Luker 1996).

Feminists cannot afford to have abortion turn into a moral imperative for some women who are poor, of color, and young while maintaining it as a choice for others who are affluent, white, and mature. The political right has kept feminists and their supporters focused on protecting abortion rights, so much so that they may have lost sight of the need to protect women's right not only to terminate an unwanted pregnancy but to birth and raise children in healthy and safe environments. A less flattering interpretation is that some feminists share the class and race privilege and biases of political conservatives. In general, feminists have failed to adequately address the needs of homeless mothers as they continue to characterize abortion solely in the language of choice—a language that denies the complex circumstances of homeless mothers (Solinger 1998). Unless feminists provide more active support and backing for women trying to mother under difficult circumstances, we will continue to estrange marginal women, who often see some aspects of their lives appreciated more fully by conservatives. For instance, some homeless mothers may feel more sympathy from antiabortion conservatives who express care for each and every fetus. And these expressions play on the real fear that homeless individuals and their children might otherwise be treated as disposable beings.

Many clients described relations with social service workers or other professionals in which they felt they were being discouraged from carrying a pregnancy to term because of some type of social status (age, race, income, and so on). For example, consider Jane's experience at a clinic during her second pregnancy:

> I was embarrassed to go to my doctor and have a pregnancy test, so I went to Planned Parenthood and it was positive. And do you know that they gave me the information on abortions and told me that the State medical card would take care of it? But they didn't tell me that if you plan to keep your child, you should get prenatal care and that your card will also pay for that. They just gave me one option, and I was very upset about that. . . . I think they did it because I had a medical card. I really do. . . . I feel that if I went in there and paid for my visit and had money that maybe they wouldn't think the same way. And that's kind of sad because I was still working, and I just qualified for the medical card anyway because I wasn't making enough money. But I was still working.

Jane felt she was discriminated against, judged as unfit to be a parent because of her financial status. She did not feel empowered by the right to choose, the right to control her body. Instead, she felt pressured not to have her baby; she felt that others were trying to dictate her choices: "They just gave me one option, and I was very upset about that." Hence, it should not be surprising that Jane feels alienated from abortion rights proponents and instead allies herself with the pro-life movement, a movement that appears to support and validate her decision to have and keep a child she wants:

> I just have a hard time with that [abortion]. I think from the minute she has a little tiny heart that she's alive. And I really have a hard time making the decision to terminate her life.

And now even more so, now that she's a little girl. And I look at her and think, "How would I have the right to terminate her life before she had a chance? Who am I to give her life and then to take it away? That's not my choice." And she knows about abortion, and she knows that was my choice, that I, of course, had that option. And she said she's glad that I didn't make that choice. . . . It could be just that I think that God doesn't make mistakes and that when people become pregnant . . . we are not the ones to take it away. . . . I feel that way. And I guess I just have enough faith that you know things are gonna work out and that my children will be provided for. . . . Angela [her daughter] hasn't had to sleep outside yet, and she's not gonna have to.

Part of the difficulty is that the pro-life movement has effectively produced confusion, remorse, guilt, and despair around abortion and then given women a way to avoid such potential turmoil (Hartouni 1991). Women can "save" their babies. They are offered the moral high ground. This leaves pro-choice proponents in either of two positions: one, of obscuring the complexity of how pregnancy is experienced by women and thus alienating women who expect abortion to be "just another option" but then find it complicated and sometimes disturbing; or two, of addressing the complexities and running the risk of providing even more power to the right wing. A feminism alert to the distinctive life situations of diverse women will maintain abortion as a legal and safe option but will also respect and support women who do not make that decision.

The notions of choice and consequence in current understandings of reproduction tie into middle-class conceptions of family planning. Here I refer to *family planning* not in its unexamined usage as shorthand for birth control but as an ideology of individual strategizing for future success. The very notion of planning suggests a kind of self-control, self-assurance, and reflection that is the emblem of the proper middle class. To plan is to be forward thinking, to take responsibility for your future. Accidents, irretrievable mistakes, and unexpected responsibilities are reserved mostly for those who are irresponsible, out of control, and unreflective, those who are contained by the immediacy of their lives rather than looking toward the future.

While clients I worked with generally did not "plan" their lives in the manner idealized by middle-class norms, the notion of planning and making conscious decisions did exist. But it tended to have a rather different slant from the popular conception of a "planned" family. For example, consider Melanie, a thirty-six-year-old white woman. Melanie met her first husband, Jeff, when she was nineteen and he was sixteen. He had just gotten out of juvenile detention hall. He had been sentenced for stealing cars and other forms of burglary. Not long after they started going out, Jeff was caught stealing cars again and was sentenced to five years in prison.

Melanie moved to the city where the prison was so she could be near him and visit him regularly. He pressured her to sneak drugs in to him, which she did, although she never "felt good about it." She never got caught. While Jeff was in prison, he asked Melanie to marry him. She said she wanted to wait until he was released, but he told her, "Now or never." Melanie was twenty-two years old when they were married in the prison visiting room:

> They just set up the date and I got the license. . . . They clear out all the chairs in the visiting room and they have the guy . . . the minister or whatever he is. I rented him [Jeff] a tux and got me a nice dress, and we had to have two witnesses, and of course there's the guards and stuff. But he's not shackled or anything like that. And we just had the wedding or

whatever you call it. And then we got to sit for fifteen minutes
and talk, and that's it [she laughs]. That's the wedding right
there. But after that, he was doing better and got in the release
center and got passes. And that's how I got pregnant with
Duke, which we planned, I planned, we both planned. It
wasn't by accident. We wanted to have a son, and it ended up
being a boy, too.

Melanie's pregnancy was planned in the sense that it "wasn't
an accident," but it was not planned as part of a middle-class
strategy of home ownership and job security. It also did not
turn out in the way she expected. During her pregnancy, her
new husband began to get out on three-day passes. He returned to burglarizing, heavy partying, and drug use during
these releases. He implicated her by both dealing drugs out of
the house and storing stolen goods there. When she was four
or five months pregnant, Jeff was arrested again during one
of his visits and sentenced to additional jail time. Although
there was some evidence against Melanie as well, she was not
charged. So he was still in jail when it was time for her to deliver. Clearly, this was not part of the plan:

> I came up there [the prison]. . . . I was almost ready to have
> Duke, and I shouldn't even have rode up there on the bus . . .
> but I wanted to see him and he wanted to see me. I got up
> there, and he told me he didn't want anything to do with me
> anymore. He wanted a divorce. He couldn't handle the whole
> thing. . . . I couldn't believe it. I was in shock. I was just totally
> upset bad. And I knew it wasn't good for the baby.

Melanie stopped communicating with Jeff for a while, even
though he called her and denied ever having said those things
to her. Two months after her son was born, she filed for divorce. However, three months after that, before the divorce
proceedings had really gotten under way, she came home to

find her window broken and Jeff sitting in her front room. He had been released from jail unexpectedly.

Melanie tried to maintain her marriage with him, even after she found out that he was seeing two other girls, who were thirteen and fourteen years old. Jeff became more violent:

> He liked to wrestle around a lot, and he'd get mad at me and he'd choke me, but I could usually get his arm away from me. . . . But once he got into jail, he pumped, he lifted weights and was real strong and big. He started throwing things at me after he got out of jail. . . . He'd always miss, but he started like punching me and stuff in the arm. . . . This is at the same time he was getting into crack, so that probably didn't help matters any. . . . And I started doing it, too.

It is tempting to treat Melanie's supposedly planned pregnancy as a mistake. She got pregnant at the wrong time, with the wrong person, under unfavorable circumstances. However, such a judgment presupposes that Melanie had the option of raising children under middle-class conditions; it assumes that the idealized version of a "planned" life will someday be available to her. To say that her pregnancy was a mistake not only disparages Melanie and denigrates her child, but it projects illusory conditions into the background of her life. Should Melanie take all the blame in this scenario? Is it just a poor decision on the part of an individual woman? Or are women in poverty more susceptible to relationships that become unstable and violent because of the circumstances in which they live?

The circumstances of Melanie's life exist in the details, in the particular accidents and specific pressures she faces within a larger horizon. These make it unrealistic for her to project radical changes in those circumstances. We must attend to the details without forgetting the horizon, as those details vary from individual to individual. The clients I worked with do not allow for the glorification of poverty; their stories do not romanticize the "hard yet simple" life. Rather, they press us to consider how material poverty intersects with idealized notions of the self-sacrificing mother to disempower women whose lives deviate from those of middle- and upper-class women.

We need portrayals of these women that do not sanitize their lives, because in an era of punitive characterizations and policies toward marginal sectors, sanitized presentations mostly open the door for others to represent the unseemly stuff even more dramatically. Close attention to the complexity and ambiguity of concrete lives might enable us to effectively counter regulatory trends, challenging the basis of stark formulaic contrasts that divide individuals into absolute categories: deserving/undeserving, innocent/guilty, good/bad, and independent/dependent. Further, such considerations may suggest how policies that offer genuine opportunities and adequately address basic needs while allowing for self-esteem, personal growth, and empowerment can create more productive results than the punitive and regulatory ones currently in vogue.

3. Precarious Lives

Drugs / Violence / Childhood / Mothering

> I had used cocaine for a long time and snorted it, and I got a
> hole in my nose and then quit. So then I started freebasing
> it. . . . We used to just go get high, but then I was like de-
> pressed and hyper and, you know, like cocaine can mess with
> you. It makes you really paranoid, so if you're not feeling like
> "Oh yeah, I'm all pumped," you can get really depressed. . . .
> And the bad thing about cocaine is you can be sitting on the
> floor, just digging around thinking that there's rocks on the
> floor, and there's really nothing. But that's how bad it is.

Here Michelle, a twenty-year-old white woman, describes
using drugs when she was twelve and living in a group home
for troubled teenagers. Unhappy, she ran away from that home
and was eventually picked up by a pimp (Byron) who physically and sexually abused her:

> He used to use objects on me, like forks and knives and hot
> curling irons and hot irons and like that. Up me [she was still
> a virgin], because I wouldn't have sex with him, and he used

to try to put clothespins on me; he would pull on my nipples
to see if they would come off. I mean he was just really cruel.

When Michelle tried to escape with the help of another
pimp, who promised to care for her, Byron caught her and
threw her down the stairs. She was badly hurt, eventually
ending up in a hospital. Her parents and the Children's
Services Division (CSD) were notified. Michelle's mother
agreed to take her back into custody: "She only wanted me
because her youngest daughter was beat up by a Black guy.
'Oh, they're all terrible.' That's what she was thinking." But it
was difficult for Michelle to live with her mother:

She'd try to punish me, but because I hadn't had her taking
care of me and doing discipline all my life, her word didn't
matter. If she said, "I'm gonna slap you," I'm saying, "I'm gonna
slap you back." I didn't have any respect or any discipline from
her at all, except when I did it was a beating and that's when I
was little. . . . [Since then] she hadn't been there for me at all.

Michelle's parents divorced when she was a year and a half
old: "Then I stayed with my mom . . . until I was four and
then I moved in with my dad. Actually, my mom just dropped
me off at my dad's. . . . I stayed with my dad until I was six or
seven, and then I was put in CSD [foster care]." Michelle tells
a complicated story about how she ended up in foster care
and group homes. She said her biological mother persuaded
her to sabotage her father's relationship with his second wife.
So Michelle "acted out" against him:

I would put stuff in his way [he was a paraplegic confined to a
wheelchair], and I would say mean things like, "Why do you
do this to me? Why can't you and mom get back together?
I really hate you because you don't do anything for me." I
wouldn't mind. . . . I tried to poison him once by putting rubbing alcohol in his coffee.

According to Michelle, her father became overwhelmed by her rebellion and decided to get help from CSD. She claims that the agency told him that the only way they could intervene was if he claimed that he physically abused her, even though he did not. So he signed papers to that effect, and Michelle ended up living in various foster homes for most of her life until she was eighteen.

"And how come your mom couldn't have custody of you?" I asked Michelle.

"'Cause she didn't want it," she said flatly, making eye contact with me.

"She just didn't feel like she could do it?" I asked.

"She just didn't want me. That's what she said then, so . . ." Michelle broke off, shrugging her shoulders and looking away as she sipped on a Diet Coke left over from the night before.

In effect, Michelle, now an adult, believes that she was placed in foster care because she was "bad," thus rendering her parents either unable to or uninterested in maintaining custody. And since she blames herself for being placed in foster care, she may also believe on some level that she deserved the troubling and debilitating experiences that ensued. Michelle had numerous troubles in foster homes:

> The first one I remember was the worst. . . . She [the foster mother] was, I think, in her late forties, and she had three kids of her own. And she had an older son, too. . . . He used to come around and slap all the foster kids.
>
> "There was a bunch of you?" I asked.
>
> "Yeah," Michelle replied.

Michelle continued:

> It was me and some other girl and then a bunch of boys. And you know, I guess the state sends you, or sends the foster

mom, a certain amount of money a month for like clothes and personal hygiene. She would go and spend like a little bit of that money on us and then she would spend the rest on her kids. Her husband was very, very physically abusive of us, and her older son touched me and another little boy there [sexually] a couple of times. And when I told my caseworker about not wanting to be there, he would come over to check the place out, and nobody would be there, and Jean [the foster mom] would just give him an "Oh, she's doing a good job, she's a good kid," you know, being nice. And afterwards, she'd be all on our ass talking about, "You shouldn't be having him come over here and check on you like that."

Michelle's description of the foster home is disturbing. The abuse and the anonymity in which she lives with "some other girl and a bunch of boys" suggest an inadequate and unsafe arrangement. She understands the arrangement in financial terms. She has a roof overhead because the state pays the foster mother, and it is to the foster mother's benefit that she allow Michelle to live there. Michelle, in return, is expected neither to ask for anything nor to voice dissatisfaction. The person who has control over her everyday life reprimands her for asking her caseworker to evaluate her living situation. The foster home, then, sounds similar to the troubled home life from which she came—if not potentially worse.

Some time later Michelle disclosed the sexual abuse she had been subjected to by her biological brother while still living in her father's custody:

It happened when I was five until I was seven. But I held it in for so many years, and then I told my dad and my mom. And my dad went to CSD, and I had to tell them that I was sexually abused. But see, my dad remembers when I was little and I came back from a home visit at my mom's [where her brother lived], and I was complaining that I was sore down there [her vagina]. And my stepmom checked me, and she said, "Tom, come here," and I was stretched out of shape and was swollen and red. And my dad said, "Did anybody touch you?" And I said, "No." And he was going to take me to the hospital but he didn't, because he said that I said that no one touched me. And he said he regrets that to this day.

"Had your brother warned you not to tell anybody?" I asked. She responded:

> My brother told me that if I told, my dad would hate me. And my dad was the biggest part of my life. He said my dad would never speak to me again and that he [her brother] would try to hurt me or my family. . . . But I wish I woulda told my dad 'cause then I probably wouldn't be in the situation I'm in now. I probably would have had it all dealt with.

"How would it have changed your situation now?" I asked her, sitting in her noisy transitional unit located on a busy road.[1] Michelle sat on the worn couch next to me. She was eight and half months pregnant and had gained fifty pounds with this pregnancy. She was a heavy woman to begin with and told me that many people still could not tell that she was pregnant. She has a smooth baby face but also a temper that I have seen flare on several occasions. The shades were closed in an attempt to keep the hot summer sun out. Her boyfriend, Tony, and their three-year-old daughter, Marissa, were asleep in the next room, and since there was no door I could see their mounded frames on the bed. They never stirred, even though we talked past noon.

Michelle told me they had had a late night the night before, which had been Marissa's third birthday. Earlier that day, I had celebrated with them in the park, along with a couple of family members. Michelle had invited several staff members and clients to the get-together, but I was the only one who showed up. I bought Marissa a lifelike infant doll for her birthday after an internal debate on my part in the overwhelming Toys R Us store. I wanted her to have the doll but worried that I was spending too much money and that it might make Michelle and Tony uncomfortable, since they could not afford such things. I also worried whether a doll was something that active Marissa would enjoy. But since her mom was pregnant and due to deliver soon, I thought Marissa might like her own "baby" to take care of.

I need not have worried about whether Marissa would like her gift. She screamed in joy when she opened it and almost began crying in her emotional frustration as she tried to get the doll out of its complicated packaging. She did cry when I went to throw the box away. She grabbed it out of my hands, cradling it and the torn wrapping paper as if it too were a baby. I no longer had second thoughts about spending the money on the doll or about the political correctness of socializing this child in traditional feminine norms. Marissa did not put down the doll all day and fell asleep with it, her mother told me.

Michelle took a sip of her flat soda, left over from when Tony walked to the store at 2:00 A.M. to get it for her, and shifted her pregnant belly. She lit a generic cigarette and replied to my question about how her life might have been different:

> If I would have talked about my abuse with my brother, I don't think I woulda had to go into treatment. I don't think I ever woulda got on drugs. And I probably wouldn't be in the situation I'm in now, you know. I mean, I'm not saying I regret it, but I probably wouldn't know Tony. I probably wouldn't have had Marissa. I probably would be almost graduated from college or in my junior year of college. 'Cause I was supposed to graduate when I was seventeen. And I probably woulda went straight into college after that.

Michelle understands various elements of her life to be connected in complicated ways. She knows sexual abuse affected her future profoundly. But she also conveys a sense of how contingent events and fateful decisions with unforeseen consequences intrude into these interconnections. It is not that one thing leads to another with ironclad necessity. Rather, each experience is connected to others in the way a loosely woven cloth is made of innumerable threads: each element would lose some of its force or significance if pulled out from the others. But social scientists, journalists, welfare workers, and political leaders tend to skate over the role of timing, contingency, and fateful decisions in the lives of the marginal women they categorize. Is it illuminating, for example, to talk about Michelle's addiction without talking about her sexual abuse, her relationship with her parents, her years of being shuffled through Children's Services Division, and understandings of her own perceptions of guilt, blame, and uncertainty? Is it also possible to make these connections without patronizing and pitying her?

My hope is to consider the ways in which lives are woven together out of numerous parts and to suggest that the dissociating of certain aspects of these lives encourages obscurity rather than clarity. The circumstances of Michelle's life from childhood on placed her in daily settings where she was surrounded by drugs, violence, and uncertainty. She is not sure whether she was loved by her parents, both of whom gave her up, and she doubts whether she is worthy of love. She blames herself, "I acted out. . . . I tried to poison him once."

As I have tried to illustrate through the section headings in this chapter, the experience of drugs, violence, childhood, and mothering are crucial to understanding the lives of many homeless mothers. Yet the way those categories are typically deployed needs to be reconsidered. In each subsection the words *violence, mothering, drugs,* and *childhood* are repeated in shifting orders. Through this technique I try to display how these diverse and interconnected factors enter, with variable intensity, timing, and effect, into the lives of homeless mothers. Drugs, violence, childhood, and mothering are necessary factors to consider if we want to understand and respond to poverty and homelessness. However, the most familiar ways in which these factors are understood and interpreted are inadequate to the actual experiences of the women involved. The representation of these issues typically renders the subject in one of two ways: either as a victim of outside forces beyond her control or as an agent of conscious and free choices who should be held entirely responsible for her life circumstances. Both of these models are inadequate. Rather, our public policies and social characterizations need to recognize how women in homeless circumstances navigate their lives as limited agents negotiating contexts with difficult and painful dilemmas.

Bureaucratic agencies tend to treat each factor (drugs, violence, mothering, and childhood) in isolation so that the issue becomes one of addiction *or* violence *or* childhood neglect. The interpretive and political task, then, is to stay alert to the interconnections between them in ways adjusted to the lives of individual women. Personal narratives demonstrate the impossibility of talking about one of these factors without the others seeping through, and the fateful role of timing and accident in shaping a life. While it may be possible to foreground a particular issue, it must not be at the expense of denying the significance of others currently relegated to the background.

Consider the political spotlight on a social problem such as illegal drug use. Part of the reason drug abuse is so villainized is that it is associated primarily with marginal populations already denigrated by the culture at large. For example, studies have shown that drug abuse is not significantly more prevalent among low-income individuals than it is among those in other income brackets (Roberts 1991, 1434; Paltrow 1992). However, mainstream representations of drug abuse suggest that it is almost exclusively an issue of the "underclass." Furthermore, particular drugs associated with marginal groups, such as crack cocaine, are presented as more powerful and more threatening than their mainstream counterparts such as powder cocaine. However, studies also show such distinctions to be false, with significant pharmacological differences between crack cocaine and powder cocaine remaining unproven (Gomez 1997); moreover, the main difference in usage patterns and addictiveness is most likely explained by the social conditions of typical users (Reinarman and Levine 1997).

Race and class discrimination pile more negativity on the representation of drug addiction (Roberts 1991, 1996; Paltrow 1992; Daniels 1993; Reinarman and Levine 1997). For example, Lynn Paltrow points out that in cases where race was identified, approximately 70 percent of women who were prosecuted for drug use during pregnancy were women of color, even while studies indicate that illegal drug use, among both pregnant and nonpregnant users, is approximately the same across race and class lines (1992). Reinforcing this point, political theorist Cynthia Daniels notes: "Although white women and black women were equally likely to use illegal drugs or alcohol during pregnancy, black women were almost ten times as likely to be reported to the authorities for drug use" (1993, 127).[2] Thus, it is crucial to address how the cultural definition, regulation, and penalization of people in difficult situations often help to generate or solidify the very results such interventions are supposed to correct. For those who are perceived as likely to transgress are often predetermined as appropriate recipients of punishment (Daniels 1993; Roberts 1991, 1996).

Addiction receives a certain cultural hype partly out of contrast between the addict's "dependency" and the independence projected onto the "normal" individual. This is done first by abstracting the normal middle-class individual out of the regular set of supports in which they are situated, and second by forgetting the role that immediate gratification in the domains of entertainment, sex, food, and recreation plays in those lives.[3] Perhaps the figure of "the addict" depends in part on forgetting those conditions of sustenance, support, and gratification the rest of us take for granted.

In *Cocaine Changes,* Dan Waldorf, Craig Reinarman, and Sheigla Murphy (1992) explain how the hype about crack's ultra-addictive power feeds a cultural desire to find chemical rather than social causalities for urban ills (see also Murphy 1992; Reinarman 1995; Reinarman and Levine 1997). However, these authors posit that a crucial factor in personal drug use is one's level of investment in conventional life rather than explaining it as entirely chemically motivated. If one receives little sustenance from cultural conventions—for example, love at home, active possibilities for entertainment, a satisfying job, school, and positive future potential—one is likely to seek compensation elsewhere. Without such stakes in the culture, a lot less binds one to the conventions of everyday life (Waldorf et al. 1992). If it feels as if you have nothing more to lose, then the high is a gain not a depletion.

Michelle's story emphasizes the need for wider public understandings of and supportive interventions in the associations among drug abuse, childhood experiences, violence, and mothering practices under difficult conditions. Then we might ask whether the experiences in Michelle's life and her negotiations of them reduce her stakes in the pleasures or disciplines of conventional life. And further, we might question, what allocation of responsibility is appropriate to such circumstances?

Michelle's troubles continued as she went to several group homes for children. In one foster home she lost "enormous amounts" of weight because the foster mother was "anorectic" and did not provide adequate food. She was also physically abused in several more homes. Such experiences in state-sponsored programs, which are designed to protect children, suggest not only failures in the system (certainly not isolated judging by the many similar stories I have heard from other clients as well as those currently emphasized in the media) but also a certain state complicity in pain. Michelle's life may not have been ideal before, but state intervention did not stabilize, nurture, or protect her (Appell 1998; Toth 1997).

So the description of Michelle's drug use that I opened with perhaps takes on different meanings as the details of her story unfold. Drug addiction is not something layered on top of a life; it cannot be peeled away while the rest of the life remains intact. In order to adequately address women's drug addiction, we need to examine how drug abuse becomes folded into their everyday lives, joining and compounding complicated lives of love, pain, hope, violence, mothering, and childhood. I cannot say precisely why Michelle started using drugs. However, it is certain that the other difficulties and violence in her life contributed to these results.

Mothering/Violence/Childhood/Drugs

Terry, a nineteen-year-old part-Dutch and part–Native American woman, had just given birth to her second child. Her husband, Carlos, had been arrested on several charges of assault against her and for having sex with a minor. He was put in jail to serve a short sentence, even though Terry testified on his behalf in court, "humiliating" herself in front of the judge. Terry looked off in the distance as we talked in the empty agency building. The usually frenzied day shelter was quiet this Saturday, the afternoon light coming in through the barred windows of the cluttered room.

> TERRY: I couldn't look at my daughter [her newborn]. I couldn't look at her eyes. I couldn't hold her. I breastfed her because I forced myself to. I wanted to give them both up for adoption because of what they were going through, Braley [her two-year-old son] even. I didn't want to give them up, but he was a mess. He was living through hell. It was a mess. I don't remember most of what happened. I go back to my dad's at some time. I begin drinking again. I begin doing lines again. This is when I relapsed. . . . . I don't remember most of this period. I know a lot happened.
>
> DEBORAH: Is Carlos with you at your dad's?
>
> TERRY: I don't know. I don't remember. I'm out of it. I have lost it. I have completely lost it.
>
> DEBORAH: Do you know who was taking care of the kids?
>
> TERRY: I was—basically on instinct. But I didn't feel for my daughter. I didn't have an instinct for my daughter. You know with Braley—with kids—you have a certain instinct. At least I did. Instinctively, I was able to take care of Braley through thick and thin. [But] I didn't have instinct with my daughter. I couldn't look at her. I couldn't take care of her. It scared me.

In some ways Terry has redefined instinct. We often think of it as something innate, precultural, a drive generated by a biological code that resists social modification. More specifically, maternal instinct is often characterized as an inherent drive that makes women love, nurture, and protect their children. It is a force that makes women both want to bear children and want to care for them above all else. But when Terry says she was taking care of her children "on instinct," I think she refers less to biological innateness and more to the experience of being on automatic pilot. In a life that has become chaotic and distressful, motherly activities are performed as lifeless routines, without thought or positive affect.

Terry's second use of the term *instinct* refers to her relationship to her second child: "I didn't have an instinct for my daughter." Here Terry may be using *instinct* in place of the words *love* or *bonding*. She did not feel an immediate love, desire, or bonding for or with her newborn daughter. Instead, she had to force herself to care for her child's basic needs. In the distress and pain of domestic violence and drug addiction Terry was unable to give herself to her daughter in a way that she had learned is supposed to be instinctual. She is disturbed and frightened because she does not automatically feel the things she is expected to feel for her daughter. Her concern about her lack of maternal feelings comes from identification with a cultural image of what a mother's response to her newborn child should be. And regardless of whether those "instincts" are defined as biological or as cultivated feelings of maternal love, to not feel them is to be at odds with her own identity.

While projects to denaturalize cultural phenomena abound, maternity may be one of the remaining places where instinct is invoked as a precultural force. Or at least maternity is often treated as if it hovers in an obscure place between the innate and the culturally generated. Consider, for example, the "bonding theory" that Diane Eyer discusses in her book *Mother-Infant Bonding: A Science Fiction* (1992). Eyer describes the way that psychologists, medical practitioners, and other members of the scientific community postulate that right after birth women are "hormonally primed" to accept or reject their infants (3). They assert that if women are placed in particular settings that promote maternal bonding at this crucial moment, it will deter future difficulties, such as child abuse and neglect.

Paradoxically, as Eyer points out, while bonding theory

appears to give women more control over their birthing experiences, paving the way for policy changes such as allowing families and infants to stay with women right after birth, such theories ultimately introduce new regulations and scrutiny of mothers (2). Medical practitioners have begun to see it as their duty not only to facilitate mother-infant bonding but also to enforce it:

> Bonding research reduced women to automatons who behave the way they do, not because of their capacity to reason, their complex psychology, or their economic or social circumstances, but rather because of their inherent and inevitable inferiority. This inferiority then requires the full services of science and medicine to guide it. (6)

Thus, the maternal side of female life is rendered precultural, controlled by instinct and hormones. But the very instability of the maternal instinct renders women unreliable and susceptible to intensive regulation. I ask, what kinds of social policies might honor women's complex circumstances in a way that supports mothering without enforcing further social control and defining women by biological arguments? Perhaps the sense of being out of control in one's life fosters parenting practices that feel more obligatory and rote than chosen and satisfying.

Terry's life experience encourages her to see mothering as a culturally engendered set of practices and feelings, while she also displays a residual sense of instinct as biologically wired. She suggests that in her case, because of the particular experiences that accompanied the prenatal period and early days of her child, she did not acquire a strong feeling of identification with her daughter, Serene. Nonetheless, she says that "it should have." Does she interpret herself to lack an instinct normally wired into those who give birth? Or does she think a mothering instinct is itself closely bound up with a set of cultural experiences that bring it into being? Her conflicted feelings suggest that she is inclined to share a larger cultural picture of the mothering instinct as biologically wired in, while her own experience with this baby calls that reading into question.

Consider the circumstances under which Terry's "instincts" were formed and cultivated with respect to Serene. Terry became pregnant after she and Carlos had reconciled and were living with their one-year-old son, Braley, in West Virginia. Carlos had "cleaned up his act." So after there had been no domestic violence for nearly a year, Terry agreed to marry him.

Things soon became troubled again in their relationship. A man in the neighborhood accused Carlos of stealing, and the neighbor began threatening the family with violence. They were so frightened that they no longer felt they could stay in their apartment. They began sleeping in the backseat of their car, even though it was the middle of winter. At this point Terry found out she was four weeks pregnant with Serene. One night Terry begged Carlos to let them all return to their apartment in spite of the neighbor's threats. She was feeling sick from her pregnancy and was worried about Braley out in the cold:

> [Carlos] didn't like that very much, so he starts racing all over the place. . . . It's snowing and we start slipping and sliding. I'm waiting to go off a cliff. [It's] the same thing he used to do—he used to threaten to run us into a pole if I was gonna leave. . . . He drives up to this cliff, slams on the brakes, and stops. . . . He starts threatening to drive off the cliff. . . . Braley's in the backseat, and I'm scared. He's being very reckless. And my stomach starts cramping really bad. It starts hurting. I say, "Carlos, please, I can't handle this. I'm afraid this is gonna start hurting the baby."

Finally Carlos stops and drops her off at the apartment. When he cools off, they decide on the spur of the moment to move to California. "We said, 'The hell with this, let's go to California.'" Such a move might seem somewhat irrational from the outside. The desire to escape from pain and turmoil often seems to take a form that might produce further instability. Yet a spontaneous move to California might seem to offer Terry and Carlos at least the hope of change, an imagined new beginning.

So Terry, Carlos, and Braley abandoned their life in West Virginia and drove across the country. Terry was sick most of way. She experienced heavy cramping from her pregnancy, and they stopped at several hospitals during the trip. The doctors told her that she was in danger of losing the baby and that she needed to reduce the stress levels in her life and stay off her feet. Carlos ignored their warnings, and because of the control he wielded over Terry, she effectively ignored them as well.

They arrived in California homeless and broke. They began receiving services through a local homeless family program and managed to find an apartment in Terry's old hometown. But this new residence did not provide much of a fresh start. Terry continued to be in false labor throughout her pregnancy:

> I was cramping so bad. I couldn't get up. I couldn't move. I would just sit there and cry. . . . And it hurt so bad. I was so scared of losing this baby, but at the same time I don't want this baby born into this. Look at this life. Look at this one [Braley]. My God, he's a mess. . . . Braley's about one or two and begins to be very out of control, very obnoxious. . . . He was a brat. . . . He was horrible. He would go into his room and rip up everything he could. He would get peanut butter out of the cabinet and smear it everywhere. And I'm laying on the couch . . . and I couldn't get up. I would just sit there and

cry and watch him. . . . And he would be so angry. He would turn around and tell me, "I hate you!" And I loved him so much. And all I could really do was let the bath fill up so my stomach could stop cramping long enough to give him a hug. And Braley would come in and he would rub my stomach. He would cup water in his hands and pour it over my stomach. He knew I was in a lot of pain. . . . It never stopped. It woke me up at night. I wasn't sleeping. I wasn't eating. There was no food. I was eating maybe every two days so Braley could eat every day. Carlos would sell all the food stamps to go get drugs. He was never there or just there to destroy the place and to be abusive to Braley. He'd come [home] long enough to make Braley take a nap, hit his butt with a paddle, then leave. . . . Or he'd come home and I'd be sleeping and Braley would be sleeping and, "You lazy bitch, get up!" And I would just cry and say, "Honey, it hurts, help me." But he would just leave.

The violence escalated. Terry kicked Carlos out on numerous occasions but continued to let him return each time. His abuse of her and Braley continued. And she knew he was dating a thirteen-year-old girl:

He doesn't come home one night. I go out and I find him and Candy [the thirteen-year-old] in the back of the car. I lost it. I opened the back of the car very quietly 'cause they're asleep, and I started punching. That's never been me. I've never been violent. It was always the worse he did, the better I did. . . . I had integrity. I was moralistic. I was good. I was really trying as hard as I could to be a good wife and to be a good mother, and I did everything I could to do right. I did a lot wrong, but I never did anything out of vengeance. But I started punching. . . . I was aiming at his cock. . . . We're fighting down the street. . . . I'm still pregnant. Candy's dad finds them in our alley and pulls out a knife. . . . I say, "Kill him! Kill

him!" This had never been me. He stabs him in the knee and
Carlos drops. . . . I said, "Finish him!"

Candy's dad did not "finish him." And Terry ended up letting Carlos back into their apartment and helping him with
his wounds. Her attachment to him and to the image of herself as a good wife and good mother makes it hard for her to
maintain boundaries from Carlos. Indeed, Terry seems bond-
ed to Carlos by what political theorist Wendy Brown calls
a "wounded attachment." She is caught in a bind: her "past
cannot be redeemed unless [her] identity ceases to be invested in it" (Brown 1995, 73), and she cannot cease to be invested
in that relationship without giving up important dimensions
of her identity as a mother and spouse.[4]

Eventually, the police arrived and arrested Carlos on
charges of assault against her and statutory rape of Candy.
During the stress of the sentencing period Terry gave birth to
Serene—a fact she forgot to mention—telling me only that
she went on Prozac because she was "literally losing it." I expressed surprise that doctors would prescribe it while she was
pregnant. "Oh yeah, I had just given birth," she explained.

So when Terry says she did not have a maternal "instinct"
with Serene, that she could not look at her, that she had no
love to give her, we might try to think beyond the presumption
of a maternal instinct that is wired in and becomes thwarted
only because of some deep lack in the particular parents.
There are cultural scenarios in which a feeling of identification and care develop. And there are cultural scenarios in
which such identifications are profoundly ambiguous, or impossible, or too dangerous to subscribe to (Scheper-Hughes
1992; Tsing 1993).

Terry's life was so filled with anguish and danger that cele-
brating a new life was beyond her. She experienced this pregnancy primarily as a cause of pain and psychic ambivalence.

She reflected on the current troubles in her life and questioned why she should bring another person into this world, while the cultural prescriptions of motherhood she participated in made it difficult to endorse her own hesitations. And so her ambivalence toward Serene—in fact, her distance and resentment of her—may be integral to the very circumstances in which the child was born. And yet one must at least hesitate to respond to this dilemma with further regulations of women. Medical interventions, such as those promoted by "bonding theories," may reduce women to being objects of discipline and surveillance (Eyer 1992); they do not address the kinds of circumstances in which women like Terry give birth to their children. A more adequate social response would be to support women's struggles to secure personal safety, psychological well-being, and economic independence.

Terry's relation to motherhood is one issue posed by her experience. But numerous identities are being produced here. Terry put it beautifully when she described herself in relation to her husband: "It's always been the worse he did, the better I did." She tries to meet the standards of a "good wife" and "good mother," but her relationship and the context in which it is set make this virtually impossible. Terry has become a martyr in these contexts. Her martyrdom provides the adjectives she uses to represent herself: *moralistic, filled with integrity,* and *good.* Terry kept taking him back because she felt "guilty," and because he "needed" her. Both Terry and Carlos embody a role defined by the other in this negative dialectic. In Terry's case, her traits are culturally valued and cultivated in women. Yet they are also lethal.

Shortly after Serene was born and Carlos went to jail, Terry left California. Before she left, she bought her husband a bus ticket down south to use when he got out of jail in hopes that if she made it easy for him he would head that way instead of following her. Terry headed north with her children to Portland to stay with her longtime friend Tommy. Tommy was also from California and had witnessed much of Carlos's violence against Terry. He had supported her emotionally and had defended her from Carlos when he could. Tommy had a place to live in Portland when they first arrived, but it was an unstable situation, and shortly after their arrival they all had to move out. Terry and Tommy became romantically involved, and this new family configuration moved into a low-budget weekly motel room. Originally, Terry had $1,200 to get set up, but she lost that and all their important documents (license, birth certificates, and so on) after accidentally leaving her bag at a phone booth. The situation became increasingly precarious:

> Carlos was calling me and threatening me. I don't know. Somehow we [she and Tommy] worked it out. I don't remember. We got an apartment. Drugs became a very large part of my life. I lost it. I'm not on Prozac anymore. It was costing me $65 every two weeks and I couldn't afford it. . . . I'm doing drugs, I'm losing it! . . . I have no love left in me. . . . I feel black.

Terry sighed, her voice winding down to a whisper, her brown hair curling a frame around her face, which looks a little older and harder as she tells this story. I wonder to myself if she wants a cigarette break. She doesn't take one.

TERRY: Drugs have now consumed my life, and Tommy's.
DEBORAH: Was Tommy doing drugs when you first got here?
TERRY: Yeah, and so was I. So between the two of us, forget it. We were out there.
DEBORAH: How hard was it for you to balance doing drugs and trying to take care of Braley and Serene?
TERRY: Very, very difficult. . . . I put rules on myself. No more than three days up, you know. I would try to keep Serene in a

clean diaper. Keep them clean. You know, I had to give them a bath every day—that was one of the rules. I just had nothing left to give. I did all the actions that I was supposed to—they were fed, they were safe, they were clean—but they weren't loved. . . . I had nothing left in me.

When Terry describes setting rules for herself about her drug consumption, such as "no more than three days up," she presents a counterimage to the portrayal of drug addicts as completely self-absorbed and irresponsible. Here, she attempts to control the deleterious effects that her habit has on her children. In this way, she discloses a struggle, and a life exceeding the cultural categories in which it is conventionally set.

Medical sociologist Sheigla Murphy, in her work "'It Takes Your Womanhood': Women on Crack," discusses the prevalence of mothers who negotiate ways to care for their children while using drugs:[5]

> Despite tremendous obstacles, many mothers—at least some of the time—manage to attend to the business of mothering while finding time to smoke crack. Experienced users knew what happened when they started smoking crack and they planned around it, just as social drinkers might plan to get their chores done before going out to a party. . . . This maternal restraint did occur and was more prevalent than popular images of crack mothers would lead one to believe. . . . Being a crack user and a mother involved protecting children from the consequences of drug use.
>
> Mothers did not really combine the two identities of mother and drug user but, rather, struggled to maintain their separateness. (1992, 153–54)

The delicate balancing act that both Murphy and Terry describe is risky business. In precarious circumstances, even while women try to protect their children from the repercussions of their drug use, such protections may be only partial and temporary. Nonetheless, the recognition of such attempts illustrates how some women attempt to navigate the pressures in their lives and exceed the categories in which they are contained.

Terry went on to describe the escalation of her drug use and the increased instability in her life. While she was living with Tommy, he changed from being an advocate for Terry with Carlos to an adversary once they were romantically involved:

> Tommy started becoming abusive, mentally and physically. I am now full of hatred and anger. I had enough love for the world a few years ago, but I'm now full of hatred. . . . I hated it. I wanted out. I got very depressed. I didn't get dressed. I didn't open the windows. I didn't do anything. The only thing I did was get up and cook breakfast so the kids wouldn't bug me half the day for food. That's all I did. I didn't clean. I didn't do nothing. Smoked. I wanted to quit drugs. I knew I was relapsing. I knew it was destroying my life.

Drug abuse, depression, and domestic violence combined as Terry hit "rock bottom." She describes the bottom of her pain:

> Finally, Tommy comes home drunk at about three in the morning. He comes in and he starts hollering at me and screaming and holds me down, screaming, yelling at me. He bit my back and then comes at my face and starts biting my face. I'm so scared of his bite. And I'm begging him, "Please don't bite me, please don't bite me." And he's spitting on me, yelling at me, screaming, and it was horrible. He gets up, and he goes and destroys the house yet again. . . . And then the wonderful thing happened—believe it or not—he hits me across the nose with the dresser drawer. The only reason why it didn't break my nose is because it hit cartilage. The scars

have recently gone away, but it was dented in for quite a while, and I looked like Rudolph. It was horrible. He goes to jail. And that's when things started turning around.

In Terry's life the visibility of a scar, as evidence of violence against her, offers the possibility for relief. Getting hit across the nose with a dresser drawer becomes "a wonderful thing." Her relief is evident from the beginning. "Finally," things got so bad that there was nowhere to go but up.

Tommy goes to jail briefly and then into a drug rehabilitation program. He tries several times to reunite with Terry, but she resists. Eventually, she decides to trust that he is changing and agrees to be his friend. He now maintains sobriety, but Terry is using crank (methamphetamines that are smoked in ways similar to crack cocaine).

> TERRY: Well, finally after a binge I go sober. I show Braley. I went and I said, "I'm gonna quit drugs."
>
> DEBORAH: You said this to Braley? [I ask this, trying to imagine how this conversation could possibly make sense to a three-year-old. But then I was forgetting what this child had gone through for his life to date. I also did not recognize, at first, Terry's need for a witness.]
>
> TERRY: I said this to Braley. And Braley's mad at me. He's telling me this. And I'm like, "Okay, I'm gonna quit." I've just come off a six-day binge, and I'm about to lose it again. So I go and I buy a bag. All right, I've broken my promise, and now I go and buy a bag. I'm on crank and I was drinking a lot, too. So I'm sitting there, and I'm chopping up. I was smoking it, getting ready to put it in the foil and smoke it. "No!" I scream this to myself. I call Braley in the room and I showed him what it was. I said, "Braley, this is what you're mad at me about. This is drugs." And I showed him everything. I showed him what everything looked like. And I said, "This is what you do with it." So we took it over to the sink and we flushed

it down the sink. And I broke the razor and threw it in the trash. I threw everything away, my mirror and all, everything gone. "That's what you do with drugs, Braley," I said. "No more!" And that was November 25, 1994, and I went clean.

Terry had been clean, according to her, for sixty-three days when she told me this story. She and Tommy were back together and were living in a motel on one of WCC's vouchers while they waited to go into a drug program specifically targeting Native American families. Braley was nearing his fourth birthday and Serene was nine months old.

Popular images of mothers who use drugs while parenting or pregnant present such women as defeated or self-centered monsters who care more about their drug-induced high than the welfare of their children. Such images have circulated through the media over at least the past couple of decades. But these representations actually indulge the identity needs of the middle class by inflating their own comparative levels of independence and self-reliance. This becomes apparent when you understand the roles that childhood abuse, poverty, domestic violence, and depression play in the drug use and parenting practices of someone like Terry. The most common cultural labels that apply to Terry—homeless mother, teenage mother, single mother, welfare mother, and unfit mother— take on one appearance when they are presented within a narrative that appreciates the specific effects of poverty, chance, and timing in her life. They become reduced to categories of stigmatization, or at best, crude explanations, when they are lifted from the chancy contexts in which they are set.

The image of the welfare mother who cares more about self-indulgence than parenting is set in contrast to the caring, self-disciplined mother who sustains traditional family values. Stephanie Coontz, in her book *The Way We Never Were: American Families and the Nostalgia Trap,* offers a useful

discussion of traditional family values (1992). She demonstrates how even in the middle and upper classes, the middle-
class ideal of the family has never existed intact in any single
time or place. It is an amalgam treated as if it were a former
reality that has disappeared and must be restored. Recognizing that the call to traditional family values reflects nostalgia for a world that never was might soften the stigmatization
often attached to people like Terry.

Once we recognize that this ideal family model has never
been culturally maintained, we can begin to move outside the
notion of individual family members as entirely responsible
for a family's "functional" or "dysfunctional" status and begin
to see the larger contexts in which families need to be considered. For example, one might examine the context of school
failure in the city, or marginal communities left isolated and
unsupported by the mainstream, or the relations among
drugs, suffering, and hopelessness. And by looking at these
larger contexts, one might be able to see how the experience
of living on edges—the edge of subsistence, the edge of violence, and the edge of cultural norms—produces families with
a destructive inner dynamic. When you examine a life like
Terry's in the detail of its trials, interruptions, and dilemmas
while simultaneously resisting the urge to measure it against
a self-serving middle-class model that has never been intact
anywhere, you reach a better understanding—an understanding that might lend itself to more appropriate and adequate responses by policy makers, social service agents, journalists, and social scientists. Coontz captures part of this in
her study:

> I am not arguing that the more things change, the more they
> remain the same. There have been many transformations in
> family life and social relations in American history, but they
> have been neither as linear nor as unitary as many accounts

claim. . . . Although there are many things to draw on in our
past, there is no one family form that has ever protected
people from poverty or social disruption, and no traditional
arrangement that provides a workable model for how we
might organize family relations in the modern world. . . . To
find *effective* answers to the dilemmas facing modern families, we must reject attempts to "recapture" family traditions
that either never existed or existed in a totally different context. (1992, 5)

Working with a family like Terry's as a social worker, with
all the frustrations and failures such work involves, I was
tempted to categorize her as a dysfunctional parent in numerous ways. She herself emphasized her inability to love, her
inability to give herself over to her children, as well as the
drug abuse and violence in which the family was submerged.
But Terry is not simply a bad mother, or a drug addict, or
a victim of domestic violence and sexual abuse, or an irresponsible welfare recipient, or a teenage mother, or a single
mother, or a homeless mother. While she is not fully consti-
tuted by any of those labels, she is also not explained sufficiently by layering them on top of each other. One limitation
of those classifications is that they do not move. They disen-
gage Terry's life from the particular events, timing, mistakes,
surprises, negotiations, and dilemmas that give it particular
shape.

The middle class, even those in it who are sympathetic to
their more vulnerable and marginalized counterparts, tends
to produce and perpetuate one-dimensional representations
of impoverished women such as Terry. By classifying these
women as embodiments of dependence and victimization on
the more liberal side—or of criminality and deviance on the
more conservative side—those securely situated in the middle
class are able to cement their own identities as self-reliant and

socially acceptable citizens. The categories offer both a self-serving counterpoint for the privileged sectors of society and the illusion of containment—that is, the notion that the problem is drugs, or housing, or sexual predators. The isolation of these social problems suggests a strategy for action that is reassuring even though it is ineffective and ill conceived.

Violence/Mothering/Drugs/Childhood

Recall Melanie, mentioned earlier, in chapter 2. She married Jeff while he was in jail, had her first son, and then attempted to maintain a troubled and abusive relationship with her husband after he was released. Her son was five months old when Jeff returned to Melanie:

> I tried to stick it out with Jeff, but he was just worse than ever. He was breaking into all kinds of places . . . and he was seeing some other girl, actually two other girls, and they were like thirteen or fourteen years old, and by then he was like twenty or twenty-one. . . . This one night he was laying in bed, he just came home from work, supposedly (he did not actually have a job), and he wanted me to turn this light off. I told him I didn't want to turn it off, because I was in the kitchen and it was sitting right beside him on the bed. . . . And he said, "Turn it off," and a few choice words. And I said, "I'm not gonna turn it off," and I stayed busy with what I was doing. He broke the lamp and he came into the kitchen and broke all my dishes and then he pushed me and I pushed him back, and he started destroying everything in the house. And he got me down on the bed and was holding on to me, telling me to do what he tells me to do.

Melanie fought back against Jeff until he bruised her so badly that she agreed to do whatever he wanted. She was "sweet" to him for a few days. Then, when he pretended to go to work one day, she gathered her infant and some belongings and escaped to a domestic violence shelter.

Clearly, what was at stake was not whether the bedside lamp was on or off. Jeff wanted control over Melanie; he wanted her submission. And he beat her into it when it was necessary. Perhaps Jeff demanded extreme authority at home to compensate for the absence of any authority or respect elsewhere in his life. This does not condone his behavior, but it shows the need to find new ways of working to change it. Some of the same types of stresses that pressure women, affecting their relationships to children, partners, work, and drugs, also affect men. And these men may respond with violent insistence. This combination of a male crisis of confidence combined with the lack of nonviolent coping skills often produces the kind of dangerous and volatile characteristics that Jeff displays.

Many women respond to domestic violence with more resignation than outsiders would anticipate. This may be partly because they experience some self-loathing with respect to their own circumstances, partly because they know they sometimes bait their partners, and most significantly, because women often see very few viable escape routes. Furthermore, the frequency of violence may have a certain numbing effect.

In her work with intravenous drug users, Margaret Connors points out that the way an addict perceives and hierarchizes risks needs to be understood within the contexts of their lives (1992, 1994). She notes that the threat of AIDS from sharing dirty needles, which to a non–IV drug user might seem terrifying, is so normalized within the drug culture that it barely seems like a risk. This is particularly true given that using a dirty needle has no immediate consequences, while getting sick from withdrawal or getting arrested for possession of drugs or paraphernalia definitely does (1992, 594–95).

So in Melanie's circumstances, we must consider whether the apparent risks she faces are experienced as that risky from the inside, or whether their mundaneness may serve to make them feel inevitable. In relation to other risks she faces, such as living alone in poverty as a single mother, or losing housing or custody, domestic violence might be lower on her own hierarchy of risk. In this light, Melanie's resistance—both her immediate fighting back and her escape to a domestic violence shelter—may be even more courageous than it appears at first glance. However, the term *resistance* may not be fully appropriate to her actions. Is Melanie resisting the battering here or is she participating in a violent dynamic? While women in distress often cater to their abusive partners to avoid violence, at other times abused women find themselves setting up potentially violent encounters.

Let's look at Terry again. Here Terry describes an early encounter with Tommy when they were reunited after his first time in jail and his time at a drug rehabilitation center:

> We get in this fight and I push him. I'm gonna push him. I'm gonna make him hit me.... I'm gonna make him do drugs.... I'm gonna pick a fight. And I'm gonna be a bitch.... I'm getting worse and worse. I'm gonna make it happen 'cause I know it's gonna anyway.

Terry points to a poorly understood element of domestic violence: she is testing and goading. She wants Tommy to prove himself, to identify himself as either a batterer or not. She also displays a certain perverse agency. She refuses to sit around and wait for the inevitable beating when Tommy loses control. Maybe she pushes him so that she will know when it is coming. Furthermore, when she talks about "picking a fight" or "being a bitch," she suggests that she may deserve what she gets. She takes on, at least partially, the identity

of someone who deserves to be beaten. And note how different that is from her earlier identity as a martyr with Carlos.

Tommy does not lose control this time. But the only way
Terry can feel secure that he won't is to push him to a breaking point. She wants to know whether he will snap and turn
on her. Perhaps it is a way of reestablishing trust and safety in
a relationship, at least temporarily.

The turbulence and injury of domestic violence profoundly affect the children involved. Terry described Braley as easily
frightened and rarely happy as an infant. Later, she described
him as a toddler as being out of control, angry, and destructive. Such characteristics are typical of children in violent and
unstable settings. Further, children often play a role in domestic violence dynamics. For example, I asked Melanie how
she felt about her son Duke living with violence and drug use
around them (both Melanie and Jeff were using crack cocaine
at this time):

> It scared me a couple times where I got pushed and Duke was
> in my arms. . . . That's one of the reasons why I got out of it. I
> mean, six months old and all this stuff is happening. But he
> was very well taken care of during the whole time. My kids
> have always been number one with me, I don't care what's
> going on. I mean they're first. And I thought I did really good,
> but I was upset 'cause of everything that was going on.

Terry describes a similar situation when she was still living
with Carlos and their son, Braley. She had moved with him to
Texas while she was pregnant, and there the abuse began to
escalate. She begins with a typical description of how the violence against her increased when she felt more isolated and
dependent:

> I didn't know anybody. I learned the town by sneaking out.
> He kept me: if I was gonna leave and he was there, he would

block one door with the dryer and he would block the other with the sofa, so that by the time I got something moved he would be there to stop me. So he would leave every night and wouldn't come back until 6:00 in the morning. So I would sneak out and go learn the town so that if I had to get away real quick, I could go somewhere. . . . I didn't know anybody. Most of his family, except his parents, spoke only Spanish, so I couldn't talk to them. So I leave him and move to West Virginia. I get an apartment. But we say, "Okay, we'll try it again." He comes up to West Virginia, and it's horrible. I'm scared to death. I wouldn't want to fight anymore, so I would go in the other room . . . and he would start screaming and wake Braley up. So I'd go pick up Braley and try to calm him down. Braley's scared to death by this point. . . . He's between three and six months old. . . . Carlos would break glass on the floor. I used to collect music boxes, and he slowly broke them all, you know, through time. He would break glass on the floor so I couldn't put Braley down, and he would block me so I couldn't get out. He had complete control of the situation. He could throw something at me, he could yell at me, he could hit me, he could do whatever he wanted. I couldn't put Braley down to defend myself. I couldn't put Braley down to hit him back. He knew that was my weakness.

Both Terry's and Melanie's stories show how much their children, in these cases both infants, are drawn into the world of violence. They are right in the middle of it. Their attempts to protect their children increase their own defenselessness against their abusive partners. Above all, Terry and Melanie identify themselves through the care they exercise for their children. Terry allows herself to be battered further because she will not endanger her son with the glass on the floor. Her son is her "weakness." And Melanie insists that no matter what else happened, she was still able to give priority to her children. Even if she exaggerates, this connection is crucial to her identity. Terry and Melanie attempt to mother, attempt to focus on their children, even while their own security and stability are in jeopardy. They are not single mothers parenting without support, a feat difficult in its own right. Rather, they have partners who actively undermine the stability of the family and endanger its members.

The identity of motherhood in a setting of domestic violence is not just about the ways that women try to parent and protect their children. It also plays an important role in women's tolerance or intolerance of abusive relationships, providing an impetus sometimes for leaving, sometimes for staying. For example, Melanie described why she struggled to stay in two successive abusive marriages. Here she talks about her second marriage in which she had two more children:

> I've tried everything with him, and it always has to do with the kids. I always think I'm doing good for the kids. I always want there to be a mom and dad, even though their dad isn't, like I said, the best dad. I wanted it to be mom and dad, and we all go and do things together. . . . But I mean—he's—it can't. . . . It's just not gonna work that way. It never will. . . . I've learned my lesson the hard way, and the kids, unfortunately, had to go through all this.

Melanie stayed with her second abusive husband, at least off and on, for nearly nine years. She learned her lesson "the hard way." The cultural notion that children need a father and that it needs to be their biological one combined with the stigma against single mothers, especially those receiving social assistance, is inherent in the "traditional family values" rhetoric of today. Such culturally entrenched images engender, as Melanie's long stay in an abusive marriage illustrates, "wounded attachments" (Brown 1995). Women often become bound up with states of injury they also seek to escape

(Brown 1995). Melanie's attachment to a fictitious notion of the "traditional" family presses her to maintain a destructive relationship. Such attachments—coupled with threats from partners, pressure from family and community, and the lack of support systems to aid escape—coalesce to make it extremely difficult for women on the edge to terminate abusive relationships.

Violence in households takes on numerous forms. For example, Ruth, a thirty-year-old white woman, reflects back on the warning signs that her marriage was unhealthy and that her husband was not a safe parent for their children. She describes his behavior toward their then three-year-old son, Tyler:

> He used to grab him by his shirt and slam him, up to where he had red marks around his neck. I saw him do that, and you know, I reacted. I was like a mother bear: "You touch my cub, well, you got to pay the price." . . . I grabbed him [her husband], and I blacked out. I was totally gone. . . . And he was turning beet red, or blue, or whatever . . . and I heard my son in the background saying, "Mommy, don't. Don't do that." And I dropped him. . . . I was just so full of rage and it just overpowered me. I was gone. I was like in the death zone. And I had him up there. . . . I had him this far off the ground and was just choking him, choking him to death. And if Tyler wouldn't have said anything in the background . . . he would have been gone. And after I came to, Tyler says, "Mommy, are you okay? Is Daddy okay? Mommy, you were choking Daddy. Why?" And it's like, because of you. Because I was protecting you. Because he was hurting my kids . . . and to me that's the wrong thing to do. . . . Because if you mess with my kids, you got the mother bear here that's gonna come after you. And I don't like showing that. . . . I don't like showing my bad side. . . . In fact, that's my evil twin. It's directly my evil twin, because once I react like that, there's no stopping me.

Ruth's story demonstrates how domestic violence so readily becomes insidious and recurrent. Who is the victim here? Is it young Tyler? The husband? Is Tyler being protected by his mother? Does the choking incident he witnesses after having been slammed into a wall make him feel safe and protected? Tyler clearly does not understand what is going on. "Mommy, you were choking Daddy. Why?" The world that Tyler experiences is one in which danger comes suddenly, from anywhere, for no apparent reason. Nothing feels safe, secure, or certain.

Ruth describes her "evil twin" as outside of her control. The impulse to protective violence "overpowered" her; she "blacked out." She experiences it as primal, as part of a maternal instinct. The only thing that restrains her from murdering the one who endangered her son—the one who is also the son's father—is her child's voice of dissent.

Ruth defends her violence because of the ways it is enmeshed in her maternity. Thus the context of maternal protectiveness gives her story a kind of social legitimacy. And yet she remains uncomfortable with it, perhaps because of her fear of the violent streak in herself. Or perhaps she knows that each act of violence sets up probable scenarios of repetition. So Ruth dissociates from her violence, naming it her "bad side," an "evil twin," an Other.

The pain and turbulence in Ruth's life did not begin here. Ruth grew up in a troubled home. Her mother died when she was five years old. Ruth remembers throwing herself out of an open window upon hearing that news. Her father remarried, and both he and his new wife physically abused Ruth. She and her younger brother were also sexually molested by their older brothers:

> Yeah, we did whatever they wanted because we were scared. They threatened us like you wouldn't believe. . . . I can't

remember half of the things. . . . Sometimes some of it will come back and I have nightmares. I wake up and my wrists are sore or my ankles are sore because they used bondage. They tied us up and stuff and gagged us. They would put dirty socks in our mouths so we wouldn't say anything. . . . It made me feel so dirty and so cheap to have your brothers do something like that. I don't know what they liked about it. . . . It just made me feel so bad.

When Ruth was nine or ten years old, her dad found out about the molestation and decided to place her and her three brothers in foster homes. Her stepmother blamed Ruth, saying that the abuse was her fault and that they had to go to foster care to protect the family's reputation. Ruth was shuffled through a couple of foster homes before she and her younger brother were moved to a place they called the "funny farm":

You were locked up. It was like being in prison in a way. . . . They put me in this really small room. I felt like I did something wrong. I still do to this day. I keep thinking about it. "What did I do wrong to be in this room?" . . . It's really weird 'cause they wanted you to take off all your clothes except your underwear. And it's like, "No, sorry, I ain't doing that." And then they had a [surveillance] camera in there, which I broke because I was mad. And then they give you a little mat to lay on, which I took that mat to be my security. . . . I blocked it around me and they couldn't see me.

Ruth felt guilty and ashamed. She came to believe that the abuse and the unpleasant places she was sent to were her fault. Ruth did not disclose the abuse outside her family for fifteen years. Clearly, as the case of Michelle disclosed earlier, state intervention did not protect Ruth. It made her feel like a sentenced prisoner, violated once again as they watched her from all angles and took away all privacy. Even her clothes were removed.[6] Ruth had to protect herself from her "protectors" almost as much as from her abusers.

After a couple of years Ruth was returned to her father's house, where she continued to be physically and emotionally abused by her stepmother and her father. She laments her dad's inability to love her. Nevertheless, "Ever since my dad passed away, it gets harder and harder sometimes to live or to survive because I don't have that part of my strength. Because my dad, although we've been through hard times together, he's still my strength. He's my hero, and he still is." Perhaps the cultural need to have a "hero" for a father figure—someone who supports, protects, and adores—drives her. Ruth's stories portray her father as offering none of these things. And yet her only alternative may be to dissociate from him and, in effect, to become fatherless. It might provide more reassurance to recall a glorified false father than a realistic, disturbing one.

Ruth moved out of her father's house permanently when she was sixteen. She finished high school living with her best friend and her best friend's mother, both of whom her father called "sluts." She became involved with a man after high school. They moved with her best friend into tents on the outskirts of town where they lived for a year or more picking up odd jobs. Then they all went into the Job Corps program, where Ruth studied accounting until she discovered she was pregnant. She married her boyfriend and they had a son, Tyler, and later a second child, Lily. Ruth describes her marriage as relatively solid for the first few years. Her husband worked at a number of odd jobs, such as pumping gas. He was "good" with Tyler at first. Then he started using cocaine and marijuana. He stopped working regularly, and they lost several residences because they couldn't pay their rent.

When Tyler was six and Lily was four, Ruth found out that her husband had been molesting them. It came out when he molested a neighbor's daughter that Ruth was babysitting and the child told her parents. Ruth confronted her husband and he admitted to molesting all three children. Ruth threw him out and pressed charges against him. Over the course of the court proceedings, she also found out that he had had an affair with a man who had since died of AIDS. Both Ruth and her children have tested negative for HIV so far.

> Well, I took him to court and . . . I almost strangled him. They had to put me in handcuffs, 'cause when I saw him, I reacted. But the judge didn't do anything. He said, "Okay, that's all right, I understand." . . . I was strangling him and he was turning purple when the cops pulled me off him. . . . He got six counts on my kids alone and for penetration of Lily to a certain point. He didn't damage her hymen, . . . but he damaged on the outside where, if she gets old enough to have kids, I might be a grandma and then again I might not. And that really hurts me that he would do something like that to destroy something that's so precious.

Ruth's sense of guilt is strong because she did not detect their molestation. She did not protect them. Perhaps one reason she missed signs of the abuse is that her own background might make those signs seem familiar, normal. For some survivors of abuse, symptoms such as Lily's nightmares and Tyler's ability to vividly describe male ejaculation may simply be what childhood looks like. "I thought I was protecting my kids," she told me one afternoon as she recounted various stories to me, sniffling from a cold in her tiny, airless apartment. "I guess I wasn't protecting them good enough. . . . I still feel guilty. I think I'll feel guilty for the rest of my life."

Ruth was in the program the entire time I worked at WCC. In many ways she was a success story. She received temporary housing from WCC and then was able to move into public housing. Ruth attended WCC workshops, went to counseling for herself and her children, brought her children to the programs for kids, and followed through on case management. However, just before I left Portland, Ruth was threatened with an eviction notice from her public housing. She was alleged to have been allowing a man to stay with her, which is against her housing contract. She later found out that this man had recently been released from jail after serving a sentence for child molestation. Success is precarious in this zone of life.

How should we interpret this event? As I go through the stories I have collected of poverty, abuse, neglect, violence, addiction, and emotional turmoil, no framework of under-standing seems adequate. The social work language is gener-ally one of "cycles." Cycles of abuse. Cycles of poverty. Cycles of violence. And indeed, the introduction of another abusive man into this family does seem to indicate a circling back over the same destructive ground. But cycle may be an in-adequate metaphor. A *cycle* suggests a predictable, seamless movement from one incident to the next, in a circular mo-tion. It suggests a trap you repeatedly participate in making for yourself. But it misses the place of accident and mistake in setting and securing traps, as well as the role of hope and pos-sibility in helping people to push against those traps. It also misses complex psychological dimensions revealed in these stories, as when an abusive childhood is thereafter linked with love. Above all, it misses the role played by legitimate in-stitutions, norms, and cultural conditions in fostering these conditions. Furthermore, sometimes each cycle is seen to ro-tate on its own axis, gliding over the ways, for example, that abuse can set you up for poverty, and then abuse and poverty can set you up to be a recipient of violence, and all three can implicate you eventually in your own bursts of violence.

We need a perspective that includes more room for messi-ness and uncertainty—one that sees pain coming from mul-tiple sources, and one that appreciates how surprise and eruption can themselves become sources of entrapment. We need to ensure that no generic account is allowed to become too uniform or closed, remembering how an escape hatch sometimes opens for a brief moment and how one is sometimes closed down by a new fortuity. How sometimes an unavoidable fit of rage can engender destructive consequences for self or others that last a lifetime.

Another limitation of the discourse of cycles is that it connects action too closely to specific consequences. It ignores how the same action in one context of social support and reinforcement can drift away, but if set in a context of poverty, uncertainty, and general distress, it might trigger awful effects (Nunez 1994). The language of cycles separates "issues" from lives. But lives are not lived as sets of issues. These lives occur within tumultuous relationships, unstable routines, desperate hopes, thin successes, and settled frustrations.

As I have tried to suggest through the organization of the sections in this chapter and its headings, it is often not feasible to talk about or respond to "domestic violence" or "drug addiction" or "mothering" or "abuse" or "childhood." These events are enmeshed in the details and fortuities of living. They often engender one another, with some screaming in the foreground now, while others whisper in the background. If we try to impose neat categories and formulas, we misrepresent those we want to portray, and we shortchange people we might otherwise support. We must allow one story to bleed into others so that a more sensitive and fluid understanding can be built up of the role of chance and contingency in difficult circumstances without reducing this complexity to a set of generalizations. Then it may become possible to fashion multiple responses to the crisscrossing patterns of homeless mothers in distress.

4. "Patches on the Wound": Politics and Dynamics at Westside Community Center

Entanglements, Negotiations, and Porous Categories

Let me begin with an ending. My return to California from fieldwork after a year and a half in Portland was not a smooth and simple one. My partner, Benjamin, and I had decided somewhat suddenly to separate. Returning to California seemed my best option. But even though the decision was amicable and filled with good intentions, the breakup was not easy.

Social work had its advantages those last few weeks. It is absorbing work, and my entrenchment in the lives of others made it more difficult to think about my own troubles. So I was glad to be working. Things were tight at the office. We had lost several staff members, and the agency was doing some reorganizing and relocating of people to different sites. The Homeless Family Program (HFP) felt rather "bare bones," and we wondered out loud to each other if we were bearing too much of the burden from the growing pains in the organization. As Miranda, the drug and alcohol counselor, put it to me one day, "The HFP has always been the bald-headed step-child." What she meant is that of all the programs at WCC, we always seemed to receive the least funding, the worst facilities, and the least attention from the administration.

On a Tuesday, after one of several sleepless nights in a row, I spent the morning working with a new family, preparing them to move from a motel where we had vouchered them to a family shelter. This move would save the agency the $300 a week it cost to keep the five of them in a rundown motel room with a microwave oven that never worked.

Then we had a staff meeting in which morale was at an all-time low. People complained about the lack of staff coverage, and Sandy, who had recently been made a program supervisor, delivered a new schedule basically abolishing the flexible hours we were all accustomed to. This change was designed to ensure that there would always be at least two staff people in the building when we were open—a basic safety rule. But it obviously affected people's schedules, making them angry and frustrated.

Then I received a phone call from a friend who had promised to help me out during my transition back to California. She couldn't do it. My composure evaporated. Choking back tears unsuccessfully, I interrupted Sandy during a meeting and told her I had to go home, that I just couldn't work right now. She stood up, trying comfort me, but I held her at bay—sobbing out final words of instruction about what needed to be covered on my schedule for the rest of the day. She nodded, murmuring, "Don't worry, don't worry. We'll take care of everything. Just go home. Don't worry." After I grabbed my coat and made a dash for my car, I somehow found a slip of paper with Sandy's home number on it in my hand. I left the building crying. I stopped at the 7 Eleven, bought a pack of cigarettes (a habit which I had quit long before), and went home to cry and smoke in the Portland drizzle.

The next day pulling into the parking lot at work I felt nervous and embarrassed. I did not want to face a lot of questions. My exit had been uncharacteristic and unprofessional, to say the least. Jared, my colleague and friend, was standing outside the building smoking a cigarette when I pulled up. I avoided eye contact with him. I think I hoped that if I pretended that nothing happened, everyone else might play along, perhaps preferring not to get involved in a colleague's personal life. Another friend who is a secretary in a corporate office told me once that when she was going through her divorce and struggling with the pains of separation, everyone in her office preferred to ignore it. But then social work is not exactly corporate work. This is crisis work; we confront issues all day, every day. The division between personal life and professional life can become quite murky.

Jared met me at my car door. "Are you okay?" he asked, looking me in the eye. "I was worried about you after the way you left yesterday."

"I'm fine," I said, feeling closed. "I'm just having some personal problems at home." Jared caught the "personal" part and let me off the hook. He said to let him know if there was anything he could do.

I had to cover the receptionist's lunch hour for my first hour at work, so I could not hide in my cubicle as I felt inclined to do. I was right out front. Sandy was the next to approach me. She reminded me that we had employee counseling if I was interested and told me she was available to talk if I wanted. Then Miranda came up, walking over with her no-nonsense approach. She got right in my face asking me, "What's going on with you?" The tone of the question virtually demanded a genuine response, although she did not push me when I evaded it. "My door's always open—you know that, right?" she said. Later I saw Margaret, our program director, who was having her own troubles (her partner was battling skin cancer). She had not been around the office much. She said she heard things were not going so well for me and that we were overdue for one of those long meetings/lunches that we did on occasion. Just seeing Margaret for the first time in a few days eased my mind.

I kept my troubles to myself. But that day, rather than scattering to their individual locations, everyone sat around during the lunch hour in the chairs next to the reception desk where I was covering the phones. We talked about work stuff and our everyday dramas at WCC. The normalcy of the stories, complaints, crises, and the company soothed me. I knew I was being cared for.

Later that night as I reflected back on the day in my field journal, I remembered the way everyone had approached me. I laughed. "Today, I was the client," I told Benjamin. "I got referred to counseling; several questions made it clear that not only was it okay for me to tell them what going on, but they downright expected me to; and [I got] countless reminders that their doors are always open." Benjamin laughed, too. But I knew that I had happened upon something new. I had seen all of those people work with clients before. But I had never experienced what their different approaches felt like. Each approach was distinctive, a variety of personalities infusing, complicating, and pluralizing the social work model. And each was powerful, directive, and genuine.

Of course, I did not receive the full client experience. The power dynamic was different. I was not pressed too hard, and I had an apartment to go home to. I did not need money, resources, or referrals in order to make it. I was not in imminent danger of living on the streets with my children or facing violence in my home. Furthermore, these were people I knew. Still, this experience offered me further insight into client–social worker dynamics; it also illustrated how this line is often blurry, more porous than commonly imagined.

If the distinction between client and social worker is sometimes unclear, so is the distinction between ethnographer and informant. In traditional anthropology ethnographers are supposed to observe but not become, examine but not embody. However, some anthropologists have recognized the value of getting "caught" (Favret-Saada 1980), a concept that Susan Harding adopted to describe the productivity—perhaps inevitability, if one is truly engaged—of entering into worlds, lives, and languages that are not our own originally but that we come to at least partially embody. In her article "Convicted by the Holy Spirit: The Rhetoric of Fundamental Baptist Conversion" (1987), Harding begins by retelling a story of leaving a lengthy interview with a reverend in the community she studied and having a near car accident: "I slammed on the brakes, sat stunned for a second, and asked myself, 'What is God trying to tell me?' It was my voice, but not my language. I had been invaded by the fundamental Baptist tongue I was investigating" (Harding 1987, 167). Rather than resisting or denying this invasion, Harding comes to understand it as a critical aspect of her ethnographic work: "I was given to think my credibility depended on my resisting any experience of born-again belief. The irony is that this space between belief and disbelief, or rather the paradoxical space of overlap, is also the space of ethnography. We must enter it to do our work" (178). As Harding points out, such experiences of getting "caught" can deepen and refine self-reflexivity and cultural interpretation. It need not be shunned or rationalized away.

In my own fieldwork, my somewhat unusual position of working in a sustained manner at a social service agency allowed me to experience such entanglements quite viscerally. In social work, getting caught may be part of what constitutes the work. Thus, my own accountability and everyday commitments to performing social services necessitated that I would partially become that which I set out to interpret. Indeed, perhaps we need to try to write the subject into ourselves as actively and persistently as we write ourselves into the subject. And perhaps this becomes more possible when it is clear to everyone involved that we do not entirely escape some of the entanglements faced more dramatically by those we write about.

That afternoon one of my clients, Gail, came up to me, her youngest in tow wrapping his chubby arms around my legs. She looked concerned. "I heard something was wrong with you yesterday. Is everything all right?" I leaned down to tousle her youngster's hair. "I'm fine, just having some hard days," I said, smiling at her. She gave me a quick hug. "I hear you," she said, gathering up her food box and her three other children as she headed out to the bus stop.

People Work

The work culture at WCC creates an atmosphere where the dailiness of lives, both of staff and clients, is recognized as relevant. Everyday lives, the strengths and the injuries, resonate through the office and enter into the work. While this phenomenon is not unique to social work, it does seem to acquire more intensity in a work setting organized around crisis intervention.

It supports a common sense strangely absent in large governmental social assistance programs that dailiness and care would underscore a program like WCC. Staff often speak about what they do as "people work," prioritizing social relationships over bureaucratic policies, paperwork, or any responsibilities that take them away from direct service connections. Indeed, the more bureaucratic aspects of the job, such as keeping up with case files and filing for various forms of financial assistance, are resented by staff, even though they recognize them as somewhat inevitable.

Staff perceive their jobs to be primarily about building relationships, relationships of trust, communication, and understanding. While they recognize the need for these relationships to be professionally contained, the nature of crisis work means that they hold more intensity than professional relations in many other forms of work. From the time a client enters the program, staff begin committing themselves to immediate concerns—usually "Where will we sleep tonight?"—as well as larger, more complex issues about the experiences, decisions, accidents, and disasters that brought a family here and what is needed to get them on more stable ground.

Staff begin by doing a long intake with a client. On the first day a client is often overwhelmed and exhausted, and so the intake is done in abbreviated form until they have been rejuvenated with food and sleep. Staff meet with clients frequently when they first enter the program, usually several times a week. And if they are being put up in a motel, staff will often meet with them there as well as at the agency—all part of a campaign to build relationships quickly and intensely.

Staff coordinate services with each other; this is part of how they build a variety of perspectives on a client and also how they balance individual strengths and weaknesses. For example, when I worked as a parent/child specialist, Jared, who felt that his understanding of child development and parenting was limited, referred all his new clients to me, and I would share my impressions and recommendations with him. Sandy, on the other hand, who was more confident in those arenas, only referred families that seemed to have persistent and serious troubles in those areas. Case managers knew who had particular strengths and called on them when necessary. So when I became a case manager, I often relied on Jack, the housing coordinator, and Sandy to help me access employment and housing referrals and to negotiate the rules and regulations of other agencies who might assist clients. In turn,

I was frequently called on, particularly by male coworkers, if there was a question of domestic violence.

In this way clients had the opportunity to build connections with a variety of people at the agency and were able to shift, either formally or informally, to working with whomever they felt most comfortable with or confident in. However, while clients were encouraged to work with a variety of staff, staff struggled to maintain a unified front so as not to get played off each other by clients. For example, if the drug and alcohol counselor mandated that a client attend her support group, a client could not expect to turn to her case manager and have this mandate reversed. Even if the case manager disagreed with the counselor, this would be discussed and worked out privately so that the client experienced only one consistent message and did not become embroiled in staff conflicts or use them to their own ends.

A great deal of emphasis was placed on teamwork and building respect among the staff, something that was often quite challenging given the divergent views and backgrounds that made up the team. Under Margaret's direction, it was acceptable to disagree among ourselves as long as the decisions we shared with clients were consistent and maintained. In many ways, building consensus was one of the most challenging but also the most fundamental aspects of the work.

This challenge grew out of the diverse orientations and understandings that brought staff to social work in the first place and that influenced how they conduct their work. At WCC there are at least two currents of personal faith discernible in the work of the staff. Generally speaking, some workers are inspired by a particular set of religious beliefs; others pay homage to a secular ideal of help and rehabilitation; and some take various elements from both sources. I will briefly outline these two faiths as a means to characterize some of the challenges and advantages of building a team out of diverse individuals.

The place of religion is critical in understanding the work lives of some individuals at WCC. This is not too surprising, given that the "helping profession" has long been tied to charitable activities and is often enmeshed with various religious organizations (Gordon 1994; Katz 1986; Schein 1995; Hirsch 1989). Even though WCC is a nonreligious organization that frowns on the presentation of religious themes or symbols at work, many staff members are deeply involved in the Christian church. One coordinator at another site is a nun. And, Barry, the program assistant and day shelter monitor, relies actively on religious values to motivate his work and guide his interventions. He frequently referred to religion in discussions with clients:

> I've always wanted to know "why I gotta be here?" I'm working two jobs, you know, and it's like, I've got my own family. I'm just that close from getting on to doing better things or to pay that last bill, but then something always comes up and derails me. That's always been the case with me, and I've always wondered why. But now I'm starting to realize, I think there must be a need for me to be here and help those in need. . . . I guess I call more on Him for help. . . . Maybe if everything was going great I wouldn't even be doing that. . . . But I do like the results that I'm able to help when I can. And I'm able to search for my strength in ways, and I try to get that across to the families sometimes.

Barry draws on his religious faith to accept his struggles. He has worked hard to make it financially and to support his children. Faith in God appears to give him both the strength he needs and the acceptance of a life filled with difficulty. There is some comfort if his life is "meant to be" this way. The belief helps him to help others. It wards off resentment, perhaps of the uphill battle he faces.

Barry believes in using religion as a spur to revive strength and integrity in clients. His religious paradigm encourages him to interpret client issues as the result of the breakdown of "traditional family values." Indeed, when I asked him why there were growing numbers of homeless families, he replied:

> I think that people didn't realize the fact that the breakup of the family was a major, major thing, you know? The fact that society has demanded more and more from people and families. . . . I really think the breakup of the family has caused a lot of the things that are happening around today—homeless families, youth having to be parents now. And in my case I find my strength in religion. I see a lot of people preferring not to go that route. But in my case I just think the key is the family, and I think it's been overlooked.

Barry's reference to traditional family values is rather generic. He talks about "the family" as if it were once a unified and concrete entity that is now splintered and decaying, an image more mythical than actual (Coontz 1992). For example, he describes "youth having to be parents now" as if this were a new phenomenon. Yet young women have been having children for countless decades, and treating teenage parenthood as a social problem is a recent production in our cultural ideology (Coontz 1992; Solinger 1992; Luker 1996).

Miranda, our drug and alcohol counselor, also identifies strongly with Christianity. At one point during a meeting with a client, they both got down on their knees and prayed together in the office. Another of her clients, a mother of five, found out she was pregnant from a casual boyfriend and considered having an abortion. She was disturbed by criticism from her family, who accused her of contemplating "baby killing." She went to Miranda for counsel. Miranda told her that she too was against abortion on moral and religious grounds. Miranda's antiabortion stance may have made this client feel that everyone surrounding her was against abortion. And so it is important to consider how religion and ethics seep into social work dynamics.

Religion is a complicated issue in a nonprofit organization such as WCC. On one hand, it is artificial to try and eradicate its existence altogether since it plays such an important role in the lives of many staff and clients. On the other hand, the long history of missionaries and their less powerful constituents (the poor, slaves, immigrants, and so forth) contains so many examples of manipulation, control, and imposition on behalf of the religion of the "helpers" (Todorov 1985) that it reminds us of how careful we must be to not recapitulate that history.

Church communities continue to provide many essential services. For example, the two overnight shelters that WCC contracted to serve families were located in churches and were staffed by volunteers from the church community. Because churches offer key elements of support, it is important to remain alert both to their contributions and to the potential problematics of the relationship between social services and religious communities. The following is an excerpt from a night-host log at one of our church shelters (the logs are written each evening and sent to case managers the next morning to inform them of how the night went):

> What a treat (*and* after undergoing *profound* spiritual crisis following the care of Jenny's family) [a client previously staying there]. I'm more blessed than words can say. I really got it that each being is a *divine creation*, no less the work of the Master Creator for insufficiencies. . . . A person is acutely needed for the spiritual companionship of hosts who hear Christ's commandments to serve the Jenny families of the earth but are left with overwhelming impotence in the face of the yawning chasm of NEED—I am serious and urgent about this!!!

This host cares for her clients because she and they are both the "work of the Master Creator." Yet she also distances herself from them because their "insufficiencies" are so profound. They are "yawning chasms of NEED." Perhaps God tests her strength by sending her the "Jenny families of the earth."

I showed this log to my supervisor, Sandy, and she responded, "It sort of makes you want to vomit, doesn't it?" I was inclined to agree. To Sandy and me the sense of superiority and self-certainty conveyed by the message stands out, while the sender of the message perhaps identifies more strongly with the care expressed in her words. Furthermore, the fear that religion may be pushed on clients at the height of their "need" is real. After I received this particular log, I spoke to my clients about this host and inquired whether they felt pressured or uncomfortable by anything she said or did. They spoke glowingly of her, saying how warm she was and how comfortable she made them feel. In the face of ever dissolving resources and minimal volunteerism, church communities remain one of the few places where people can receive assistance.

Still, coordinating with church communities can be difficult because of the beliefs they might want to impose. Prior to my work at WCC, the agency had contracted with another church to provide shelter for families. Several months into the arrangement the church realized that some of the families we sent to them for shelter were unmarried and some parents were same-sex couples. The church felt that they could not provide services to people who were "living in sin." WCC, unwilling to compromise its own beliefs, canceled their relationship with this church. The dilemma is that such religious beliefs often supply an indispensable fund of motivation to provide services to needy clients while they can also create patterns of support that exclude many who need help. The general trend away from public entitlement services to privatized services suggests that such discriminatory agendas may become more prevalent.

Sometimes the power of religion is less overt. Over the winter holidays Margaret, our director, asked Barry to take down the Christmas decorations he displayed in the day shelter, particularly the nativity scene he had put up. Barry was angered and did not understand her reasoning. To him, the clients all celebrated Christmas; why shouldn't he make the place festive for them? They have no home to go to, their children do not have a tree, and he was simply trying to make the shelter feel warm and celebratory. Margaret pointed out that such decorations may serve as a subtle sign to non-Christians that they do not belong here. They might suggest that this agency is run by and for Christians, a message she wanted to avoid.

However, while Margaret wanted to regulate the role of religion in social services, she also recognized a place for it:

> I don't think that it all needs to leave the workplace, in part because I think that religion is part of building community for a lot of people. . . . You know, you've got a bunch of blocks that you can put together and build a community. And each individual has to hold the blocks together for herself, and a great many of those people would pick up a block marked "Christianity" and put it in the puzzle. And so it's possible that having a staff person with a bible on their desk helps a person who's a Christian find that building block and put it on their table. As long as the person who's not a Christian isn't in any way put off. . . . It has to be handled carefully, but it doesn't have to be completely wiped out, 'cause then you lose something.

If the Christian orientation to nonprofit services poses some dilemmas, consider the secular orientation. I use this phrase as shorthand to think about the role played by feminism, antimarket perspectives, and social movements in social work. For example, Margaret described a previous job at a for-profit organization that provided home health care to the elderly as an alternative to nursing homes:

> My heart was definitely there, but I couldn't quite match my motivations for being there . . . with the bottom-line, capitalist venture that it was, which got me into a lot of trouble with the agency, although they kept promoting me. And actually with each promotion I was further away from helping the elderly stay out of nursing homes and farther into things like accounts payable, getting people to pay their bills, office manager, that kind of thing. . . . So I left that job after five years because I just couldn't handle it. I had come to see that something like health care didn't belong in the profit realm. And that I couldn't come to terms with trying to make money off of people's misfortunes and health care needs. . . . I felt confident that we were providing really good service, but we couldn't provide it for people that didn't have a lot of money, because it was very expensive. So I'd get calls from poor elderly that I couldn't help, and that made me crazy. I couldn't reconcile it at all. So I left with the feeling that health care shouldn't be for profit, and when I left all I knew was that I wanted to work in nonprofit.

Jared offers a perspective even more anticapitalist. He suggests that poverty issues will never be adequately addressed in a capitalist culture because

> it's against powerful people's interests. So I don't think those people who are actually the decision makers want such changes, because if such changes happen, then there is no reserve labor, [and then] if someone goes on strike, they have to give them what they want. . . . So the problem is the greed and the way the rich get richer. . . . So I think the solution would be educating people about what's going on in reality and the

division of the classes. The Contract with America is really the contract with the rich.

Jared places his work in a global economic context. He believes that the capitalist system requires the kind of underclass that he attempts to Band-Aid on a daily basis. Yet in order to conduct his work, he must also narrow his perspective somewhat, measuring his own success by those he helps to exist successfully within the limits of their lives, limits dictated by a stratified class system. He feels successful with a family when they trust him and follow through on his suggestions. His comments suggest that he focuses on small-scale success even while emphasizing its liabilities. And while he believes in antipoverty work, he does not think social services actually address poverty on the large scale that is needed:

> The other frustrating part is that we are only putting patches on the wound. In a way I think this type of social services . . . is like a steamer—you know, the pot that has a valve. . . . You open the valve to get the steam out so the whole thing doesn't explode. Pretty much that's what we're doing is opening up the valve a little bit so that people don't get too fed up. And I think that also perhaps stops the changes. People don't see homeless families in the street. They put them in a shelter and hide them. And when people don't understand the reality, the way they vote and the way they do things is not going to be effective, because they don't know the reality of what's going on. . . . I think the government is trying to hide the reality of what's going on with these families and children.

So while Jared values his work and the help he gives to particular families, he has to motivate himself to put "patches on the wound" in a setting where he is unable to address more basic issues. In fact, he points to how such work may actually mask the severity of the troubles of families in poverty and allow most Americans to stay insulated from such realities. Jared works within the system we have; he continues to work each day, after five years with WCC, serving homeless families. Perhaps his radical perspective about the larger evils of capitalism contributes energy to his efforts to reduce some of its effects in the small ways available to him.

Sandy, a case manager and program supervisor, suggests that one of the reasons why social workers take on some of the issues clients bring is that "we are caring people." That care, that desire to help is sustained in various ways by different individuals. Social workers are notoriously underpaid, particularly those in nonprofits, who work for approximately half the wages of government workers. Margaret pointed out that even the executive director of WCC keeps her salary low because of the limited resources of the agency:

> We lose some good people to the county or to the school system because they see it as a way of staying in social services but getting paid more. And that's what really hurts us because the government can pay more than nonprofits, and people feel like they're in a social work field but they can earn twice as much money. And so we lose them. And frankly, I think that sucks because that comes directly from the people, too. I mean, one of the reasons I don't get paid more and why Diana [the executive director] doesn't have the board pay her more is she has this absolute belief that for every dime we pay ourselves, we take it directly from the families.

Clearly, social workers are not motivated by high salaries, social prestige, or perks. As Sandy pointed out, we do not even have business cards. The WCC building has no frills, with two or three people in the few semiprivate offices and the others in tight cubicles. Upon visiting my brother, a business consultant, in his posh computer technology office—replete with dramatic flower arrangements, Oriental carpets, avant-garde art, a state-of-the-art sound system, and a maze of richly carpeted hallways and offices—the only thing remotely reminiscent of my workplace was the concrete service stairway.

Many social workers use their own experiences with poverty, homelessness, abuse, and/or addiction as points of reference for their work. They set themselves up as models. Sometimes their approach to clients becomes bound up with a desire to vindicate more generally the path their own lives have taken. Such a high value on personal experience as a way of knowing might offer a degree of self-validation to those who work in a field that receives little validation from the larger culture. So from yet another source, the world of social work is both complicated and enriched by the motivational sources available to its practitioners. Jack, the housing coordinator, described it this way:

> I think it's just interesting how we take our own personal views on how we think a person should get there [become self-sufficient]. You and I [could] have two exact families, and I think that they should go into job training right away and you think, "Oh no, mom needs parenting classes . . . because she's been so emotionally scarred." . . . I guess I'm . . . maybe I'm skewed by my views. . . . But that's the hard part, when it gets into those kind of values. . . . And it gets frustrating, and so I'm not necessarily—I mean, I can't fault the family always, but I kind of fault you and me because we're the ones that they're coming to, and we're supposed to lead, and so when we're doing this, it's like, are we harming or helping, you know, the family?

Personal experience can provide a critical well of knowledge, but it may also be inherently limited, too idiosyncratic, or as Jack put it, too "skewed." What about consistency? What happens if one family, by the luck of the draw, works with

Jack, and he emphasizes job training and his "just-do-it" message, while another family works with me and is subjected to what Jack calls my "rosy-posy liberal bullshit," which emphasizes positive parenting, looking at personal histories, barriers, and so on. How can social services negotiate the subjective quality inherent in the work? While formulas and cold precision do not seem an adequate response, relying entirely on personal belief systems seems risky too.

I myself was the object of suspicion and my competencies were called into question because of my assumed lack of personal experience. During my first week at WCC I met with Sandy as part of my informal orientation. She struck me as the most jaded and irritable of the staff, and I was wary of her. She looked me straight in the eye that day saying, "I hate it when they hire people based on education who don't know anything about the families we serve." Clearly, even though she had not interviewed me and knew little about my background, Sandy assumed that my life was one without the experience of poverty or abuse and that my education removed me even further from such experiences. Thus, in Sandy's mind, my lack of personal experience undermined any formal competency I might have.

Months later, during an interview Sandy revealed herself to be a survivor of domestic violence—a situation so brutal that her repeated attempts to flee eventually left her homeless with four young children. Sandy finds her experiences with poverty, violence, sickness, and struggle to be a source of enrichment to her social work:

> I think people have to almost go through some kind of trauma in their life—something that really has them facing their own reality. I mean their own love for themselves. Because I was like many who didn't think too much of myself, and I had a lot of self-hatred, you know. And I had some very destruc-

tive behaviors. So when I worked [through] that, which took a good five years—Ugh!—to a point where I could feel good about myself and feel empowered and on the right track, then things were clear. I think it's very very helpful [to have experience] so that you have some empathy for whoever you're working with, especially when you're working with very vulnerable people. Someone needs to be there that has that background, and it's hard to get there. But we all really have it because we've all had some kind of experience that relates and is connected. It's just finding it in yourself.

Sandy's insight into how she has transformed her own pain, turbulence, and self-contempt into empowerment and competence as a social worker expresses a more general dimension of staff capability and motivation. She has even softened on me a bit, suggesting at the end of her statement that diverse people can reach these levels of empathy because "we've all had some kind of experience that relates and is connected."

Barry, the program assistant, also privileged personal understandings of homelessness and poverty. He identifies experientially with clients: "Even though I wasn't never actually homeless, you know. But I'm a single parent, and I raised a couple kids on my own. And so there were issues that I had already incurred and been through, and things like that, that these people are going through."

And Jack also understands his own working-class background as shaping his approach with families: "I know that I come from the same families as the families we serve, and I've had everything they have in my family. And I've been able to pull myself up." Jack's ability to pull himself out of poverty leads him to believe that everyone has this route available to them. It contributes to his motivation to provide services that encourage self-help. However, while the other staff I worked with emphasized the "people" aspects of their work as what motivated them, Jack seemed primarily interested in finding correspondences to more prestigious and less direct-service-oriented careers. For example, he stressed his interest in helping clients determine their "rights," which he compared to being a lawyer, and he emphasized his own role as a decision maker and allocator of resources, which he compared to being a judge. These kinds of emphases allow Jack to feel good about himself while remaining detached from families: "I don't get all stressed out. I don't get worried. I mean, families come in, and they come and they go, and you know, I see you guys [the other staff members] get all stressed over, you know, maybe you're more involved in some ways. I don't get as attached."

Perhaps, then, what Sandy said earlier about personal backgrounds as a base of understanding in social work can have multiple effects. Identification does not always produce empathy. Jack's history of poverty and turbulent family dynamics makes him want to draw clear distinctions between his life now and then. And those distinctions carry over into the work setting, producing a critical, demanding orientation toward clients—one that distinguishes their "failures" from his "success." Indeed, Jack's need to dissociate so strongly may reflect fears that his own position is more precarious than he would like to admit.

Personal experience, religious ethics, and political values coalesce to complicate and generate social service work. The point I have begun to explore here and will continue to expound on in the following section is how something like social work becomes infused with the differential sources of motivation available to the staff. The identities that bring people to social work and the interpretations they use to make sense of their own lives and the lives of others are fundamental to nonprofit social services. It seems important to recognize both the positive possibilities of such personally invested interactions and the kind of dangerous, missionary type tendencies such orientations can slip into.

Internal Politics

Margaret once told me that she had a recurring dream. She is standing at the bottom of a snowy hill. At the top are numerous children of clients she has served, sitting on toboggans. Children whose faces are burned into her brain more deeply than her own nephews and nieces. They begin sledding down the hill, gathering speed, gathering momentum. Margaret feels panic rising in her as the toboggans race toward her. She stretches out her arms wide, facing them. But she cannot stop them. She cannot catch them all.

Margaret told me many times, "We are not here to save families—we are here to serve them." But the line between serving and saving is far from precise, as her dream may illustrate. Margaret wants to save those children racing down that hill. She wants to catch them. She wants to protect them from the worst bumps. But her ability to do so is extremely limited. Sandy mouths the same self-protective mottoes as Margaret: "You can't do everything for everyone. You can only do as much as you can do. As much as they'll allow you to do. And they have to do the rest."

Perhaps the single most common catchword at WCC is "boundaries." Setting boundaries allows a social worker to resist becoming so immersed in a family's issues that they take over your life. As Jack put it, "Then we've got two of us that are a wreck, and I do less of a job." This strategy of maintaining staff-client boundaries provides staff protection and can also promote respect for clients. Sandy explains:

> You cannot change someone else's behavior. . . . You can try to
> point things out to them, you can try to get them assistance,

but you can't make them do anything. So getting stressed out about it is ridiculous. . . . So you have to get to that point where you realize that . . . you're limited on what you can change, you know? And so I believe in reality therapy, and I go more for straight talk and telling people, you know, "In my opinion . . ." and "In my experience . . ." and so forth and so on. This is what they need to do to get to point A or point B or whatever. You know I'm happy to help them get there or whatever they want to do, but it's always their choice. I don't beat around the bush. So that allows me to not have that stress. . . . A lot of times we'll take that on ourselves automatically because we're caring people; otherwise, we wouldn't be doing this. And when we take it on automatically, we're taking on all their baggage. It's their baggage. They need to be responsible for it no matter how painful that is. . . . You can share some of that and that's a bonding. But you can't take it from them.

Sandy outlines two main elements of maintaining boundaries. She takes the pressure off the case manager to make something happen. In the same vein, she cautions workers against trying to control client decisions. Keeping boundaries means leaving clients to their own choices. It also means leaving them with their own issues, "no matter how painful." A worker may be inclined to take on something for a client, with good intentions of wanting to ease the burden. But the implication in that move is that the worker is more competent and capable of handling things than the client herself.

Strength-based services suggest that clients are there for services and for certain opportunities, not to have their decisions and lives determined for them. *Strength-based* basically means that the agency works from the premise of client competence and builds on strengths rather than focusing on what is "wrong" and in need of "fixing." However, I have also heard

Sandy—the purveyor of boundaries—describe herself as "motherly" with some clients. Sandy often tells clients what she thinks they should do, advising them strongly and getting frustrated if they do not follow her advice. The mother-child relationship is tempting, but it threatens the notion of strength-based services. It may infantilize the client, suggesting that because they are homeless they are incapable of making decisions and organizing their lives.

On the other hand, as a woman in her fifties with many years of social service and life experience behind her, Sandy's particular approach of "mothering" may infuse warmth into a client-staff relation that can otherwise become fairly formal. Sandy's intentions come from a place of genuine care, and she, like many other staff members, deeply wants clients to succeed. The trade-off here perhaps provokes a question without a clear answer. Is her mode of caring inherently disrespectful and thus inappropriate? Or does it have some redeeming features that make it worthwhile for some staff workers?

Jack and Sandy share the goal of self-determination for clients. However, where Sandy might slip into a patronizing, familial model, Jack strictly avoids such identifications. In this case, the trade-off is that his relations with clients lack trust and care. Indeed, Jack often suggests that other workers are getting "taken in" by clients whom he suspects of lying and misusing resources. While it is not predetermined that genuine warmth risks undermining client authority or that a strict sense of boundaries results in critical and antagonistic relations, such outcomes seem worth pondering further.

The differences between these two social-service orientations result not only in distinct staff-client relationships, but also in a complex and sometimes contentious social-service team. Staff members often found themselves embroiled in debates about strategy, approach, and client relations. These debates sometimes became heated, perhaps because both personal identities and professional competencies were called into question. In fact, Jack admitted that conflicting values among the staff represented the most significant challenge he faced at work:

> I think the biggest thing for me sometimes is when two people have opposed values. And it doesn't come from the families, 'cause I don't get into the values of the families. But I do get into the values of the people that I work with. . . . You know, I work with you every day, and I may not work with this family every day, so then I go home and I get frustrated. "God, I gotta work with that damn Deb, and do you know what she said today?" That's when I get more frustrated. . . . When our values collide. And it's like, can I come to work and still keep my values and do the same job? Or do I need to start looking and say, my values are being tested and I'm having to give up on something. It would be the same thing for you, I mean if I were to impose my values on you to where you felt you had to step away from your values. . . . That would be wrong, too.

On the surface, Jack seems to enjoy playing devil's advocate and office jokester. He is the token Republican in the office. He laughingly shares his Rush Limbaugh book with coworkers, which he displays on a shelf by his desk. And he is always up for a loud debate over welfare reform, capital punishment, or indeed, any issue involving punishment. Yet clearly the liberal atmosphere of the office challenges Jack's ideologies about work, family, and punishment, and as he suggests, the challenge sometimes disturbs his work.

Jack goes on to describe his perspective on having colleagues who are gay and lesbian:

> I get along excellent with Darren [a gay caseworker] . . . but there was a couple people in the agency that have such differ-

ent sexual orientations, and it's like this big badge. And it's like, you know, they shove it down my throat, and that's when it gets difficult. . . . You know, I don't have to invite you over to my house for dinner, I don't have to invite you to watch my kid, but damn it, I've gotta work with Darren, and if I've gotta work with him, then we better be able to do a good job together.

It is easy to portray Jack as homophobic—"they shove it down my throat"—but such labels do not entirely capture him. When this same gay man to whom he referred lost his sister suddenly and had to buy an expensive, short-notice plane ticket abroad, Jack spearheaded a drive to contribute to his ticket, saying, "We're always helping strangers [clients]. Don't you think we should help each other as well?"

Feminist values in general were difficult for some staff to negotiate. Both Jack and Barry, the day shelter monitor, expressed concerns about the effects of feminism on policies and strategies enacted at the agency. For example, under the supervision of our program director, women's needs, particularly in cases of domestic violence, were given high priority. Margaret said to me once, "It is hard not to see many of the men who come through here as just in the way." Margaret's focus on female victims alienates some male workers. Jack described feeling uncomfortable in meetings when domestic violence was discussed and anger against male perpetrators was vented:

You know, if you're a woman and you're sitting around with a bunch of guys, and they're talking about women and they're talking about sexual things—even if you know the people— you still start feeling a little bit uncomfortable, I'm sure. Well, it's the same way when women are talking about domestic violence. I know they're not talking about me. I know they're not talking about all men, but it sounds like that. So you start getting defensive.

Jack worries that the focus on women marginalizes men and shuffles them into negative and disposable categories. But Margaret believes that it is only possible to work with one party in a domestic violence situation. She chooses the victims, who are overwhelmingly women:

> I believe that with an individual family or an individual couple, you've got to choose. Like with Kristy and Joe, we can't get caught up in his needs. She's already too caught up in his needs, and that's part of why she's been his victim for so long. We needed to focus, and we need to help her focus on her safety and her strength. . . . If we had diluted our effort and attention into trying to also fix him or help him get where he needs to stop battering, there's too much risk that it would have been to her detriment.

Margaret also believes that the power dynamic in domestic violence is so stacked against women that working with both parties in a relationship in effect supports the violence. Such a policy of dual treatment might imply that past violence is condoned or that it is not significant enough to castigate the perpetrator. Furthermore, women are often so terrorized that conventional middle-class forms of relationship counseling, like communication training or mediation, can appear successful while actually serving to conceal abuse.

Jack disagrees vehemently with Margaret on this point, feeling that families are being broken up too frequently and unnecessarily under the cover of resisting domestic violence:

> I think that the whole definition of abuse is overblown. . . . I look at someone like Warren Moon, a big football player. . . . After the game was over, he went home and he was frustrated. . . . He lost it, he snapped. He grabbed his wife and just started, you know, pushing her and choking her or whatever. . . . She called 911. . . . Never happened before, hasn't

happened since. But too many women want to label this domestic abuse and say "Well, you should leave him. You know
he's gonna do it again." I worry about that. . . . I think we need
to start giving people another option. We need to start sitting
down and offering them services. . . . [If] we can save a relationship, it's a hell of a lot better than breaking it up.

Barry, too, expressed grave concerns about family values
and keeping families together. Barry's desire to strengthen
what I characterized earlier as a fictitious notion of the traditional family encourages him to downplay the issue of domestic violence and other struggles that women sometimes
face with male partners, such as the financial strain of drug
habits or nonpayment of child support. There is a real danger
in minimizing the importance of these issues. Women and
children are put at imminent risk. Furthermore, the widespread rhetoric of family values and the notion of keeping the
family together as a social priority often press women to stay
with physically and emotionally abusive men. Barry struggles
with these issues. He does not have an answer to them, but he
does think that it is essential to find some model of male
competence and self-esteem that is compatible with the safety and strength of women.

So Barry often clashed with other staff members, including me, around client concerns. He would become frustrated
in discussions about domestic violence or other forms of
abuse against women. He sometimes accused us of "male
bashing," suggesting that we forget all about the needs of men
while talking endlessly about the needs of women. I can remember him storming out of meetings on more than one occasion, his 6'5" frame towering above us as he left.

In an interview Barry equated the feminist movement
with separatist movements that exclude men entirely. He tentatively expressed this when he described the challenges and

rewards of working with a client population of mostly single women and a mostly female staff:

> I've enjoyed working with women. I like women. I love women. I like the fact that towards me they feel very comfortable in talking to me. . . . I think because I listen. . . . Women have told me they felt very intimidated in talking to another lady. The only thing I can see as a danger in having a lot of women is that you're sending a mixed signal that you don't need men, okay? And as you know, I do a lot of reading out of the Bible, and I think the importance of man is very important. I mean the right kind of man. . . . Because I don't know a woman who would not enjoy a man who you feel you can trust. A man that was living upright, not out with another lady. . . . I think men have slipped there, so there's been a lot of anger. . . . So it's like the abuse toward women by men and things of that case, I think WCC concentrates a lot on that. There's not an emphasis on the other side. I don't think we have one men's group. . . . We need strong men, too, 'cause that's one major reason why families are falling apart. . . . I think there should be more men staff. When I say *staff,* I think there should be more men in the supervision position, showing that a man can understand what a woman is going through.

Barry is wary of the feminist values prevalent at WCC. Better, perhaps, he wants to balance them with other considerations. As an African American man and a single father, he identifies with clients who struggle against discrimination, economic instability, and family difficulties. Barry worries that men are marginalized not only by the lack of positive emphasis on male clients, but also by the lack of men in supervisory positions. Indeed, during my stay at WCC we had no male program directors out of the five directorships.

It may be that Barry and Jack exemplify a larger trend. Men of color and white men from working-class backgrounds may experience feminism as particularly threatening and unjust because they feel that it doesn't recognize their own barriers and hardships. Furthermore, these populations of men have a long history of prejudiced portrayals as perpetrators of violence and crime and thus have particular stakes in calling into question and dismantling anything resembling such portraits.

The need to balance supporting women with recognizing the need to work with men is a complicated one in domestic violence work. For example, during one of my many conversations with Margaret about domestic violence I discussed the paradox of not working with perpetrators. I pointed out to her that even if one's loyalties are with the victims, to leave batterers without support services may not adequately address the issues involved. We had one case in which we helped a woman and her two children flee to another state from a violent and dangerous partner. In order to protect her and ourselves, we pretended to her abuser that she had just disappeared. The man continued to spend time in our day shelter for several more days, perhaps waiting to see if she returned or perhaps because he had nowhere else to go. I watched in frustration as he tried to get involved with a young single mother in our program. So while we assisted one woman in getting safe, we left his abusive behavior unaddressed. The chances of his battering another woman remain very high. Margaret replied:

> I need to expand my thinking on this. I was trained that if you're working with victims, then you can't work with perpetrators. Joy [her mentor on domestic violence issues] always said, "We can't take care of them—we have to take care of ourselves. . . . Your brutality is not my problem, it's your problem, [so] you take care of it. I'm going to keep myself safe." So as a body of women, or as a body of people working with

battered women, it's like a collective statement: "You're the perpetrator, you're the batterer, you're the one with the problem. You go take care of it. We're going to stay safe and strong. And we can't simultaneously stay safe and strong and help fix your problem and illness." That's very simplistic. And it's probably wrong and probably a cop-out. . . . That's why I've tried to be more open in the last couple of years to the idea of doing men's groups and the idea of moving towards being willing to work with men [batterers] around violence issues. . . . It's hard because I have no desire to work with perpetrators, particularly after working with their victims for five years.

Margaret reflects on how her perspective has been formed, where her loyalties lie, and ventures a cautious openness to change. But she also senses that the well of motivation she has to draw on is not infinitely deep. It is important not to let the well dry up. She does not pretend that her experience, knowledge, and training provide her with all the answers. She recognizes that an issue such as domestic violence is complex and volatile. We become emotionally involved in it, and that is unavoidable, even while it may also be problematic. As a social worker she tries to address it on all these levels; she even tries to address her own strengths and limitations. For example, while she recognizes that there may be a need for a men's group, she realizes that this is a service she will not be motivated to participate in. She has too much anger after years of working with victims, including one instance in which a client was killed by her batterer after she returned home to retrieve her belongings. The very identification that enables her to do this difficult and frustrating work also sets limits on the directions that work can take.

One of the ways in which those limits are stretched and those directions pluralized is by the contentious yet diversifying perspectives among the staff. While debates and differing orientations were not always experienced on a daily basis as a "productive" tension, there was a base-level respect, at least most of the time, that characterized this team. Margaret summed it up this way:

> I'm pretty convinced that there's no other field I could work in where I could have so much respect for so many of the people I work with. The field draws people that I have a kinship with and yet [who] still challenge and stretch me. Now, I don't need to work around everybody who's just like me. I like some diversity, but I also want to be around people that I can respect and who can respect me. . . . I come to work every day because I respect and like the people that I work with. And I work with some odd people [she laughs]. I mean, it's not necessarily that all the people that are around me in WCC are people that I would choose to be friends with, because there are some real odd ducks. But I respect them a lot, and I like it when it all comes together in team dynamics, and I believe that each person is heard. . . . This community has strength to bring to these problems, and that's what keeps me coming back. . . . And the courage in some of the individual people I've worked with . . . you know, it's inspiring.

In what she recognizes as an odd group and others sometimes see as a cantankerous and frustrated bunch, Margaret finds an inspiring and effective community. Margaret may be one of the more optimistic and idealistic members of the team, and Jack might dismiss her notion as more "rosy-posy liberal bullshit," but an understanding of how the interpersonal dynamics of the staff at WCC operate might offer a larger perspective on the limits and possibilities of social service models today.

Thus far I have explored the kinds of conflicts and possibilities brought to the social service setting through the makeup of the staff. In the final section I turn to the kinds of interpersonal dynamics promoted by the worker-client social positions.

A Push or a Hand

Social worker and client relationships contain a somewhat unusual mix of elements. They are policy driven, yet intimate; based in unequal power relations, yet governed by the end of empowerment; they necessitate one-sided disclosure by the clients, yet they often marshal the deepest identifications of the staff. Indeed, the very term *client* conjures up an interesting set of paradoxes. A legal client, for example, enters into a contractual agreement; the client hires a lawyer in order to serve his or her purposes. However, the client in the social service setting has enormous need and little power in choosing how those needs get addressed or if they get addressed at all. Thus, the terms of the "contract" are not terms that the social service client is in a good position to either shape or reject.

The identity of a client in a social service setting is a limited one, one that simplifies otherwise complex individuals (Kingfisher 1996). Such reductions render clients as easily dissected, diagnosed, and categorized, something the social service model demands. Some social scientists have argued that the term *client* is particularly loaded with connotations of dependency, and so they prefer to replace it with terms they find more respectful, such as *welfare recipient* (Kingfisher 1996) or *welfare reliant* (Edin and Lein 1997). Catherine Pelissier Kingfisher in her book *Women in the American Welfare Trap* (1996) makes this argument explicitly. While I am sympathetic to Kingfisher's critique of social service productions of client identities, I do not find her preferred term *recipient* any more palatable. Kingfisher notes in her research that while Adult Family Services workers refer to those on welfare as *clients*, the women on welfare prefer the term *recipient*. While this is not insignificant, I think the terms are effectively inter-changeable and that perhaps the most pertinent difference in connotation is who is using them. I have chosen to use the term *client* throughout my work, while simultaneously call-ing the implications of this category into question.

The dynamics between social workers and clients partially produce the categorical identity of "client." These dynamics demand that clients take on certain personae in order to be deemed "good" clients and thus deserving of such services in the first place. A good client is uncomplaining, undemand-ing, forthcoming with honest information, hard working, and willing to recognize what the worker determines to be the client's weaknesses and barriers to success. Deviations from this model are "challenges" to the worker. The incentive to appear to be a good client is strong since workers have enormous power over clients.

When I first started at WCC, I was shocked by the seem-ingly quick decisions to "terminate" clients who were not "following through" on their case plans.[1] The rationale is that if a client is not prepared to take the necessary steps toward self-sufficiency, then the agency is unwilling to "waste" lim-ited staff time and resources. It prefers to take on another family ready to take full advantage of the opportunity.

While it is not helpful to clients if an agency "enables" self-destructive behaviors, an individual may need more time and space to deal with their dilemmas than the agency is willing or able to give. The agency, however, is determined not to provide services that promote dependency and allow families to maintain irresponsible behaviors. As Jack put it: "I think the families that are most successful are the families that have come and maybe gotten a push but not a hand." Such a model is supposed to encourage client self-sufficiency. However, it may also determine lives through what is ultimately a punitive model. If you are good by agency standards, you get the carrot; if not, you get the stick of termination.

Consider one client's relationship with her case manager. Michelle was living at one of the agency's transitional units and had two weeks left there. She was due to deliver her baby seven days after her move-out date and had no housing prospects. Her case manager was threatening to immediately terminate the family's services because of their lack of follow-through:

> I don't feel there's any communication between us, you know what I mean? Because, I mean, Jared goes home every night after work.... He has this nice little house to go to, and on the eleventh we don't have anywhere to go.... And maybe he just doesn't see it the way we see it. Maybe he just can't understand our point of view. I mean, before Tony [her boyfriend] moved in here, he was staying with his sister. When his sister said he couldn't stay anymore, Tony was sleeping on the street.... He didn't even sleep; he was just walking around on the street. How can you look for a job when you're walking around on the street?... I can't be on the street again, Debbie.

Similarly, Kelly voiced this frustration about an interaction with her case manager:

> I don't like having to go and ask people all the time. I don't like going to WCC and begging for some laundry vouchers [which clients can cash in at laundromats] and then feeling bad about it. And that's what I have to do. [She imitates a plaintive childlike voice.] "Can I get some laundry vouchers?" And then I get that look and a big sigh, "How many?" And I'll say, "Five" [in the same voice], knowing that I really need seven, but I'm afraid to say seven, so I'll say five. And then she will say to me, "Well, didn't I just give you five?" And I'll say, "That was two weeks ago." And she'll say, "Okay, I'll give you five." And it

makes me feel terrible. I mean, I have to build myself up some energy to be able to go in there and ask for some laundry vouchers—when I should just be able to have a job, get my money, and do my laundry. It should be very simple.

Kelly feels frustrated and trapped by the interpersonal dynamics at the agency. She believes her case manager does not respect her or allow her to maintain dignity in the face of her needs. Instead, she feels she has to grovel and plead to get her needs met. Additionally, Kelly points out that even though the solution of self-sufficiency should be really simple, it's not. She has not been able to just go out and get a job. She has two young children, one only nine months old, and a partner who I later found out was abusive and addicted to drugs. So as Kelly points out, it is not simple at all. She remains in a position where she needs assistance. Furthermore, the stigmatization attached to that assistance makes her dread everyday tasks in her life and makes her feel infantilized:

I shouldn't be afraid to go do my laundry. I don't like going to the laundromat with them [vouchers]. They treat you differently. This last time she [the laundromat worker] actually got the money and brought the money out to the washing machines. That's humiliating. You know, John [her boyfriend] said, "My God, I thought she was going to go around to each washing machine and put the money in." That's embarrassing. We feel like children. . . . Was she wondering did I really have that many loads of laundry? Or was I going to take the money? . . . I would have showed her my laundry, but she didn't need to do that. . . . It's not fun going through the agencies, even though with the exception of one person [her case manager] everyone at WCC has been wonderful.

The flip side of the client concern with infantilization and regulation is the staff's concern about client manipulation.

There was great trepidation that clients might lie to a worker and, for example, cash in a laundry voucher and pocket the money rather than do their laundry. This might exemplify one way that staff enforce larger cultural priorities, determining that clean clothes are more important than whatever else a client might choose to do with the, say, $10 they gain. What if the $10 could fill up a car with gas, allowing the client to get to job interviews easier? Must social workers make such determinations? Then again, what if that money went for drugs or cigarettes rather than clean clothes? Does WCC want to subsidize this priority? Fundamentally, the staff fear being taken in or manipulated—a suspicion that perhaps underlines the power dynamic within the agency most pointedly. Staff want to feel that they have control over their resources, that those resources are being used in a "productive" and "appropriate" manner by their clients. Clients want to feel that they have control over their lives. Perhaps this perpetual conflict expresses on a smaller scale the way in which a struggle over identity is maintained in staff-client relationships. The consequences for a client who is deemed noncompliant—that is, not productive and inappropriate—are severe. When clients are cut off from services because they fail to follow through appropriately, the reality they face can be quite dramatic.

While working at WCC, I never became fully comfortable with this model. Colleagues gently admonished me for being too soft and having "weak boundaries." People worried that I would be open to manipulation because of my attachments to clients. For example, I was disturbed when Jared decided to terminate services for Michelle, her boyfriend, Tony, their three-year-old daughter, Marissa, and their newborn, Anthony Jr. Michelle had been a "difficult" client. She was self-righteous, loud, prone to outbursts of anger, rarely appreciative, and had multiple personal difficulties. I liked her a lot. And I was very attached to her headstrong and unruly daughter, who always referred to me as "*My* Debbie." As far as Marissa was concerned, I belonged to her.

After five months with the program, Tony had still not found a job and the family seemed no closer to permanent housing than when they came in. Tony and Michelle's relationship was perpetually rocky. Both seemed stuck in patterns that immobilized them. They often failed to follow through on aspects of their case plans, and many service providers had complained about them. Jared had already considered terminating their services. I had argued to keep them on the caseload many times, finding social work rationales for what I knew was mainly my own concern about what would happen if they were just set adrift. I lost the last battle, and the family was told that when that week's motel voucher was up, they would no longer be receiving services.

Since they were not officially on my caseload, I did not have to tell them this, but I stopped by the motel anyway to check in, see the new baby, and say good-bye. Tony answered the door cautiously when I knocked but let me in when he saw who it was, even though neither Michelle nor Marissa were fully dressed, having just finished a shower. Marissa, in her efforts to reach me, began leaping over the mountains of garbage bags full of clothes and other things that seemed to leave no room even for air. "My Debbie, my Debbie!" she shouted, throwing her still wet body at mine in a rough-and-tumble embrace. I hugged her tight, a little longer than usual.

I looked over at Michelle. I had wondered before I came what her reception would be. I wondered if she would be angry at WCC and thus anyone associated with it. She smiled at me and pointed to the new infant lounging in his infant seat. Anthony Jr. was one week old. I moved closer to admire him. He looked pale and sickly, with a wandering eye. His cheeks rolled into his neck, full of baby fat. She motioned for me to hold him, which I did.

We made small talk while she got herself and Marissa dressed. Tony stayed outside on the balcony, perhaps because the room was already so jam-packed, with no space for this many bodies. Michelle said she didn't know what they were going to do once their voucher came up, but she didn't seem panicked, at least not yet. She still had three days with a roof over her head. I encouraged her to keep in touch with me and others at WCC. I told her she should keep coming to the women's support group, which was open to the public, and to bring Marissa to children's group. She said she would, but I doubted it.

After a while it seemed time for me to go. I settled her new-born back in his infant seat and said good-bye, as casually as I could muster. As I headed down the Astroturf-covered concrete stairs of the motel, I heard Marissa running out after me. I waited for her to catch me and give me another of her fierce hugs. My heart was in my throat. Of all the children that I cared for during that year, Marissa, the most "difficult," was the one I wanted to take home with me. She was mine as much as I was hers.

"Be good," I told her and stroked her wet hair, sending her back up to the room so she wouldn't see that I was upset. I cried in the car all the way home. Later when Benjamin came home, I was still incoherent and sobbing on the couch. "Why did I tell her to be good?" I asked him as he tried to comfort me. "Everybody always tells her to *be* good. Why didn't I tell her that she *is* good?!" Benjamin knew that no response from him was going to be adequate. I was just going to have to struggle with the injustices and injuries for a while, and with the painful knowledge that Marissa would probably struggle with them much more intimately and longer than I.

Perhaps the decision to terminate was the only thing left to do, given the context of this case. It is difficult for workers at WCC to experiment with new approaches. While WCC prides itself on flexibility and on tailoring services to the individual, services are also confined by limited funds and staff. And while the agency desires to be respectful and accepting of clients, the demands put on it for strict monitoring of funds, the larger public pressure to protect the reputation of the center by limiting the risks posed by clients (*risk* here is defined by the behavior of clients in relation to public assumptions of tolerable behavior), and other such pressures result in an intense push to conform to prescribed norms. This is not entirely detrimental. Surely some structure is essential, and as we have seen, it is necessary to the effective functioning of the agency that it work with the diverse motives, desires, and beliefs of workers who respond to the difficult cases they are given. Yet such structures need to be balanced by the recognition of the cultural norms they perpetuate. The current entrenchment of the cultural ideologies that hold up the welfare state makes it difficult to imagine other possibilities. It is probable that only a large, sustained political reform movement could move these boundaries significantly. But perhaps studies that make palpable the complexities, injuries, and social costs of homelessness can make some contributions to the shift in interpretations and motivations needed to modify this context.

5. "Don't Feed the Alligators": Debating Welfare

Words from Washington

On Wednesday, July 31, 1996, President Bill Clinton announced that he would sign a new welfare reform bill. He declared this four years after saying that he would work to "end welfare as we know it." In 1992, Clinton promised to spend $10 billion to accomplish the goal of "empowering people with the education, training, and child care they need" (*New York Times*, August 2, 1996, A1). However, during the next four years the climate grew chillier toward poor communities, and Clinton joined more conservative constituents in attacking welfare and its recipients.[1] The new bill, I argue, assaults the poor, who serve as political scapegoats for a host of social ills that remain outside the range of concerted governmental intervention. Women and children are denied basic subsistence in this country as poverty is treated more and more as the result of personal defeat and individual irresponsibility.

The governor of California, Pete Wilson, made these remarks about welfare during his 1997 State of the State Address:

"Welfare reform offers us the opportunity and the challenge to recast our very culture, to insist on responsibility so that tax payers no longer subsidize idleness or promiscuity and no longer suffer when illegitimacy hatches into social pathology" (*San Francisco Chronicle*, January 8, 1997, A9). Wilson links the new policies to the representation of recipients as "idle, promiscuous, and pathological." In his presentation, welfare recipients need to be shaken out of their worlds of illicit pleasures and into the righteous world of wage labor: "We're ending welfare's warehousing of people who don't want to work. There's a lot more dignity in any minimum wage job than sitting on a couch collecting welfare" (A1).

Wilson seems invested in perpetuating stereotypes about the poor. He attacks welfare recipients, promoting images of the "welfare freeloader" growing fat off the labor of hard workers. Such racially coded images feed the already burgeoning anger of the working class, perhaps particularly many low-income white men. Members of the working class find themselves working hard at menial jobs, struggling increasingly to gain a decent, livable wage. Simultaneously, this population senses that it is not addressed or protected by major progressive social movements of the day. And thus they often become disaffected from the welfare state. They become ripe targets for political portrayals that scapegoat a population whose vulnerabilities might otherwise seem too close for comfort. As political theorist William Connolly puts it:

> The way the issues of ecology, racism, feminism, education, job discrimination, and taxes were defined [in the seventies and eighties] set up this core constituency of the welfare state for a hostile takeover by the American right. . . . Large sections of the working class living close to the margin faced hardships not incorporated into the agenda of national debate: a decline in the number of good jobs available to blue-collar

workers, no national health care plan, poor retirement prospects, and no effective programs to subsidize higher education for their sons and daughters. . . . The contemporary subject position of the white male blue-collar worker, then, is
well designed to foster a culture of social revenge and hyper-
masculinity. (1995, 133)

Thus, comments such as those made by Governor Wilson do
not simply mold public animosity; they identify constituencies already prepared to receive such messages and crystallize
frustrations and resentments already in place.

Consider the remarks made by Senator Phil Gramm, a
Republican from Texas, during a Senate debate on welfare
reform:

No society in history has ever invested more money trying to
help needy people than the United States of America. . . .
What has been the result of that investment? Well, the result
of that investment fifty years later is that we have more poor
people today than when we started. They are poorer today
than when we started. They are more dependent on the government than when we started. . . . When we started the current welfare program, two parent families were the norm in
poor families in America. Today, two parent families are the
exception. When we started the current welfare program, the
illegitimacy rate was one quarter of what it is today. . . . Our
current welfare program has failed. It has driven fathers out
of the household. It has made mothers dependent. It has
taken away people's dignity. It has bred child abuse and neglect and filled the streets of our cities with crime. And we're
here today to change it. (*New York Times,* August 2, 1996, A10)

Senator Gramm does an impressive job of treating welfare
as a self-contained system. All the negative effects he decries
are treated simply as products of the system itself. If the poor

are poorer today than they were fifty years ago, it is because of government assistance, not other reasons. Furthermore, Gramm suggests that taking these entitlements away will begin to reinstate "traditional American family values"—that is, the nuclear family, legitimate children, and most of all, independent citizens. "Dependence" is an effect of welfare; "independence" is an effect of self-reliance within an open system of traditional family life, employment possibility, and hard work.

The opposition between independence and dependence thus forms a key element in welfare discourse. As Nancy Fraser and Linda Gordon point out in their genealogy of the term *dependency*:

> Few concepts in U.S. social policy discussions do as much ideological work as "dependency." The term leaks a profusion of stigmatizing connotations—racial, sexual, misogynist and more. It alludes implicitly to a normative state of "independence" which will itself not withstand critical scrutiny. Naming the problems of poor solo mothers and their children "dependency," moreover, tends to make them appear to be individual rather than social problems, as much more psychological than economic. (1994, 5)

Such a concept of dependency resonates in Senator Gramm's comments. He suggests that we have done recipients a disservice by fostering "their" (read: poor women of color) dependency on "us" (read: affluent white men). So we must remedy this situation with "tough love," taking strong measures to enable them to stand on their own two feet.

Senator Daniel Patrick Moynihan, a longtime commentator on the welfare system and the underclass, is quoted by David Berris with this definition of *dependency*: "An incomplete state in life; normal in the child, abnormal in the adult. In a world where completed men and women stand on their own feet, persons who are dependent—as the buried imagery of the word denotes—hang" (in Berris 1994, 6). Here welfare dependents are represented as incomplete, stranded in a childlike state. They are deemed "abnormal," deficient, and thus a drain on the government system they rely on. They "hang" in a nebulous state—adults who cannot establish adulthood because of dependencies that belong to childhood. They are wayward, rebellious adolescents in need of regulation and tough love.

During the same debate Representative John Mica, a Republican from Florida, used a vivid analogy to characterize welfare dependency, comparing recipients to animals. During a Senate debate on reform he held up a sign that read, "Don't Feed the Alligators," explaining:

> We post these warnings because unnatural feeding and artificial care create dependency. When dependency sets in, these otherwise able alligators can no longer survive on their own. Now I know that people are not alligators, but I submit to you that with our current hand out, non-work welfare system, we've upset the *natural order*. We've created a system of dependency. The author of our Declaration of Independence, Thomas Jefferson, said it best in three words: Dependence begets servitude. (*New York Times*, August 2, 1996, A10; emphasis added)

While Representative Mica asserts that recipients are not literally animals, the image he uses does considerable work to outstrip the thin words of denial. The image of the alligator as an aggressive carnivore resounds in the background of his declarations. We do, he insists, participate in a "natural order" that has been "upset" when the government provides benefits to the poor. What natural order is he referring to? It appears to be one that says, "It is irrelevant what kind of background you have. The system will work effectively as long as everyone takes care of him- or herself in it. It fails only if too many are allowed to lapse into aggressive dependency through their own irresponsibility."

Representative Mica offers no proof for this theory. He identifies no time in history when a political economy worked without a variety of supports and supplements for numerous constituencies, including those implicitly defined by him today as "independent." Yet his message of welfare predators barely creates a ripple of protest as it enters the well-established sea of antiwelfare rhetoric.

These political logics of natural orders and the welfare system as a self-contained institution are deeply dubious. It is very doubtful that if fifty years after the construction of welfare we find the poor poorer, that fifty years after its destruction we will find them better off. So who are the alligators? Those trying to feed off the remains of the system? Or those who are ready to gobble up the poor because their very presence in the world deviates from the *natural order* of things?

Why do so many politicians put so much time and energy into attacking the welfare system and its recipients? Their political rhetoric suggests that the focus is due to budgetary concerns. However, this is radically insufficient considering that welfare accounts for, in the highest estimate, 3 percent of the federal budget—if you include food stamps and child nutrition programs (Piven 1996, 62). Frances Fox Piven asks this same question about the unnatural attention to issues around welfare in "Welfare and the Transformation of Electoral Politics." She argues that in the absence of the ability for either political party to produce policies that speak affirmatively to poverty and unemployment, both parties tend toward a politics of fundamentalism and blame:

> When people are blocked from dealing with the problems of
> livelihood, community, respect and security through politics,

they become more susceptible to fundamentalist appeals. When institutional reforms seem impossible, frustrated publics are more likely to respond to calls for a politics of individual moral rejuvenation, typically coupled with calls to mobilize against some vulnerable group. This group becomes the Other, embodying a kind of moral pollution that is to blame for the problems people experience in daily life. Something like this seems to be underway in the United States. Politicians are trying to direct popular attention away from the issues of wages and jobs to a politics of individual responsibility and "values." At the same time, political leaders are pointing to minorities and the poor, and especially poor women, as the miscreants, the polluters, whose transgressions of core values are responsible for contemporary troubles. (1996, 65)

As Piven points out, the words and actions against welfare attack the most vulnerable sectors of society. Stereotypes such as "welfare queens" and "irresponsible" and "lazy" recipients bolster the self-confidence of some segments of the working class by demonizing a segment of the population ill equipped to respond politically to these portrayals. The moral targets are picked in part because of their very vulnerability.

The politics of welfare have now become so heated that it is necessary to consider how some of these larger cultural debates intersect with the social service agency I have engaged. The rhetoric of welfare and the enactment of welfare reform in Washington mark two powerful means by which recipients are produced as particular kinds of subjects, in this case negative ones in need of tighter and more punitive controls. In this chapter I place some of these words from Washington into conversation with WCC staff and clients. In this way I hope both to exemplify how such words and ideologies filter into other sectors of life and to help to reframe the terms of the debate.

Talking Back

> I want to get off welfare. We did everything we were supposed
> to do to get off it. I want to get off welfare bad . . . never could.
> —Terry, WCC client

Many WCC clients complained to me about how much they
hated the welfare system. Few would choose it as a way of life
in the face of other viable options. The hypocrisies, inefficien-
cies, and injustices of the welfare system are well documented here and elsewhere. The question is whether those defi-
ciencies must be translated into the sort of interpretation and
policy responses expressed above. My concerns fall into two
main categories. The first addresses the economics of welfare
and its entrapment of recipients; the second explores the way
that recipients are negatively depicted and the effects of such
portrayals on their lives and their possibilities of action.

By *economics of welfare*, I mean the maintenance of families
at such a low subsistence level governed by high levels of bureaucratic hypocrisy that it is extremely difficult for families
to move from welfare to employment sufficiency (Ehrenreich
and Piven 1984; Piven 1996; Lambiase and Rule 1996; Epstein
1997; Kingfisher 1996; Edin and Lein 1997). Some studies
suggest that current welfare benefits may even promote illicit
behavior by providing unlivable incomes and denying families the right to any other means of subsistence. In *Making
Ends Meet: How Single Mothers Survive Welfare and Low-Wage
Work*, Kathryn Edin and Laura Lein convincingly demonstrate
that welfare benefits alone are inadequate for a family's survival (1997). The authors begin with the paradox that most
surveys of poor families indicate incomes well below their
reported monthly expenses. They then interviewed welfare-
reliant mothers to establish how this discrepancy is generated
and where women make up the difference. They conclude
that welfare benefits alone leave families unable to meet their

basic subsistence needs and thus require families to find ways to supplement their incomes. The discrepancy is a product of the difference between subsistence needs and welfare levels.

Edin and Lein also point to why there is a conspiracy of silence about this apparent discrepancy:

> Conservatives did not raise the question, because they did not want to draw attention to the fact that AFDC benefits were too low to support a family. Liberals were equally reluctant to discuss the issue, because they did not want to admit that recipients were balancing their budgets with unreported income. This conspiracy of silence encouraged the public to imagine that welfare recipients could get by on whatever the legislature chose to give them. Once the public accepts this comforting assumption, it becomes natural to cut benefits whenever the state budget tightens. (1997, xii)

The welfare system needs reform, then, but the recent reforms will generate more poverty and compensatory cheating (Piven 1996; Roberts 1996). There needs to be a more fundamental overhaul, one that promotes greater self-sufficiency (for self-sufficiency is always incomplete and partial) by working on the wide variety of conditions that engender the need for welfare.

In his book *Welfare in America: How Social Science Fails the Poor,* William Epstein concludes his examination of welfare studies and policy with a call for greater generosity: "The long-term remedy would seem to lie in providing all Americans with assurances of more equal participation in basic social institutions and at levels adequate to protect the nations' civic society. Yet, the nation is perversely moving in the opposite direction even while its wealth is increasing" (1997, 232). A move toward generosity does not appear likely in this age of individualized blame and punitive reforms. Epstein admits that such an orientation is unlikely to take hold until some undeniable social calamity occurs (233). Until then, we are likely to face inadequate public resources and entitlements increasingly linked to hoops that recipients must jump through in the endless effort to prove their economic, moral, and cultural worth.

Lucie E. White also discusses the ways in which welfare reform measures designed to push mothers into wage labor do not take into consideration the complexities of everyday lives for single mothers. For example, she argues in her article "On the 'Consensus' to End Welfare: Where Are the Women's Voices?" (1996) that new welfare policies do not address how women will organize adequate child care. Instead, such legislature renders these kinds of discussions parenthetical to the overarching concern that mothers "work" in a manner legitimated by the state—that is, wage labor (White 1996, 19; see also Fraser and Gordon 1994).

However, the complex lives of women in difficult circumstances demonstrate how child care is seldom simple or straightforward. It can be an exhausting and debilitating task to arrange. Furthermore, the terms of the welfare debate mean that the failure to arrange such care adequately results in punishment. Leaving children in inadequate care while the parent is working may result in loss of custody. And, of course, the double bind is that if adequate care is not arranged, a mother will lose her financial safety net, leaving families destitute.

In her ethnography *Women in the American Welfare Trap* (1996), Catherine Pelissier Kingfisher offers a striking example of an informant who was trying to get off the welfare rolls (see also Polakow 1993; Appell 1998; White 1996 for other examples). This woman began working as a prostitute, a position that enabled her to afford an adult babysitter for her children. However, when she moved from this stigmatized and illegitimate employment to socially sanctioned work, she could only afford less qualified teenagers as child care providers. The teens she hired sexually molested her children. So as Kingfisher points out:

> For Susan, trying to do things the "right way" by getting a "respectable" job turned out to be the wrong way. She learned that playing by the rules had numerous, and often unacceptable costs. As she put it, "I put my kids' lives in jeopardy to try and get off it [welfare]." (26)

The dilemmas faced by women trying to negotiate these social paradoxes are not inconsequential, as we have seen in previous chapters. The difficulties in trying to mother and work in circumstances complicated by poverty and its corollary pains are serious. As this client illuminates, "doing the right thing" in these circumstances often produces the wrong results. The negotiations between work, welfare, motherhood, child care, and child safety nets are often difficult in ways not addressed sufficiently in the contemporary terms of the public debate about welfare.

Similarly, a WCC client named Tonya attempted to get off welfare *before* all these reform measures were enacted. She found a reasonably well-paying manual labor job. Her son was four years old then, and she was a single mother, having left an ugly, violent relationship with the boy's father, who was a drug addict. Tonya had difficulty making ends meet and could not afford a day care center. She began leaving her son with the apartment manager of her building, who agreed to watch him for modest, sporadic pay. Tonya liked her son to be close to home, and since she did not own a car, it allowed her to avoid expensive transportation costs.

Several months later she discovered that her son was being sexually abused by the manager and his companion. Is this boy, whose suffering was intense, likely to become "dependent" in the future? Is he an example of the "social pathology" to which Governor Wilson refers? Is either he or his mother responsible for this result? Or is blame a useful enterprise here? For even to focus blame on the perpetrator of sexual abuse does not really help mothers in these situations to resolve the dilemmas posed by working and needing child care. Perhaps the costs of *not* addressing issues such as safe child care are higher than those of addressing it. White describes it this way:

> The logistics of planning a child's schedule is an extremely stressful task for the most affluent of two parent teams to manage. That stress can become incapacitating for single mothers with no cash, no car, no phone, few contacts, a battered self-image and only one pair of hands. Yet, when welfare reform proposals address child care, they never spell out the details of how poor single mothers can secure care for their children every single minute of their work day. (1996, 20)

The refusal to address such dilemmas means that current welfare reform legislature acts primarily as an assault on the poor, seldom providing a genuine escape route from poverty.

Even the reformers themselves are unable to show how forcing mothers to work will benefit their children. As legal theorist Dorothy Roberts points out:

> Underlying the consensus that welfare mothers should work is often the conviction that their children are socially worthless, lacking any potential to contribute to society. Welfare rhetoric assumes that these children will grow up to be poor and consequently burdens to society. The proposals dismiss any possible reason to nurture, inspire or love these children. (1996, 12–13).

Roberts investigates the racialized presentations of attacks against recipients. She argues that one of the main factors spurring animosity against welfare is the widespread belief that AFDC primarily benefits Black mothers. Roberts goes on to suggest that dominant images portray Black mothers as inherently unfit and their children as "socially worthless" or dangerous from birth. The dominant paradigm outlines no reason to support Black mothers' staying at home, according to Roberts, since *their* mothering serves no recognized social value.

As critical historians of welfare point out, at their inception welfare benefits were provided primarily to white women.[2] These poor women, primarily widows, were treated as the deserving poor—women who would have naturally been in the middle class had some specific, uncontrollable misfortune not befallen them. Furthermore, the program was set in a paternalistic frame, governed by rules that allowed screening out "undeserving" women, including virtually all people of color. However, as White points out, the civil rights movement decoded the criteria that sustained such screening and opened up possibilities for women of color to receive federal assistance (1996). This change in racial composition eventually contaminated the program's reputation, stigmatizing it as a handout for Blacks, even though Blacks make up less than half of all recipients (White 1996, 23).

The new image of welfare recipients as primarily racial minorities who are parasites of the system is one that conservative politicians mobilize and exploit, and one that the media perpetuate and sensationalize. For example, as Charlotte Ryan discusses in "Battered in the Media: Mainstream News Coverage of Welfare Reform," sensationalized cases of welfare abuse are used to feed public anger and concern, setting the stage for "reform" (1996). Ryan cites the Massachusetts case of Clarabel Ventura, a single Puerto Rican mother on welfare:

> She represented every stereotype of the welfare system run amok, starting with the stereotype of the welfare mother as baby factory. The twenty seven year old Puerto Rican mother

of six children by four different fathers was pregnant with her seventh child by a fifth man. She represented "generational dependency," that notion that welfare begets welfare. Clarabel's mother had raised 17 children, 14 of whom were now raising 74 children on welfare. She represented the stereotype of welfare mothers as bad mothers—Ventura had a history of drug addiction and her children had been removed multiple times for abuse and neglect. She also represented the stereotype of the welfare queen with Massachusetts state officials promoting estimates that Ventura and her extended family were costing tax payers close to a million dollars per year in various subsidies. (1996, 30)

The image of the poor mother of color exploiting the system for perverted pleasures, abusing her children, and wasting taxpayers' money promotes public horror—but not shock. Large sections of the public eat up these extreme images of dependency in the Other, perhaps because these very images reinforce their desires to see themselves as independent and radically distinct from constituencies that receive handouts. Such stories thus readily become the public truth about all poor, single mothers of color. Ryan goes on to say:

Media attention to the case was key. The public furor lent conservatives the steam to push forward previously stalemated reforms. [Boston] *Globe* columnist Mike Barnicle acknowledged the role of the media as a cultural actor molding public perceptions of reality: "Ventura has passed beyond the boundaries of news. Today she is part of local lore: a crack-addicted welfare cheat who allegedly burned her little boy's hands to the bones and could not stop having babies or grabbing public money. . . . Ventura has done for the welfare debate what Willie Horton accomplished for the prison furlough program, sent it crashing and burning to the basement where the mere mention of the woman's name, Clarabel, immediately invokes the darker spirits within us. Everyone getting assistance is a dirty, rotten, fat, lazy, no-good minority fraud simply intent on breeding and scamming a check, all the while laughing at the rest of us who work to support them. . . . Never mind that it is not true." (1996:30)

The racist and classist images promoted on various fronts of the welfare debates converge to create an atmosphere of disrespect, animosity, and suspicion toward poor mothers. They foster punitive policies that exacerbate the poverty and struggle that already exist, while derailing informed efforts to create public networks of employment opportunities, child care, and welfare support. Such constructions not only serve to diminish housing and income possibilities for the poor— they undermine their sense of self-worth and competence.

Politicizing, Experiencing, and Negotiating Blame

Individuals who rely on welfare benefits are caught in a web of cultural paradoxes. Their identities as independent adults, as good citizens, and as good parents are all called into question by their implication in the welfare services designed to help them. In the meantime, working adults who receive medical benefits, child care support, parental leave, and support from a middle-class network of family, professional, and friendship ties are defined rhetorically as if they were fully independent, self-sufficient individuals. The individualization of blame for welfare recipients depends on a cover-up of the multiple forms of collective dependencies in which middle-class life is set. This individualization of blame is thus doubled by the individualization of worth for middle-class people. Each mode of representation requires the other to be sustained.

For example, after working at WCC awhile, I became struck by the degree to which I adopted a cleansed or laundered version of those very conservative vocabularies I resist,

vocabularies closely tied to current paradigms of the impoverished and the ethics of social assistance. At the agency, we talk
about "clients" who need "assistance," who must attain "self-
sufficiency," and so on, endlessly. It is not so much that these
terms fail to apply. Rather, they inadvertently sustain a sharp
line of division between those presumed to be self-sufficient
and without need of assistance, and those who are cast as
needy and dependent. Consider, for a moment, a typical university professor. She probably received plenty of assistance
from her parents, her teachers, and the state in preparing to
become what she is. Even the roads she drives on, the garbage
collection she depends on, the police protection she receives,
and the eligibility for insurance she attains—all implicate her
in a complex system of dependencies and assistance (for
other examples see Coontz 1992).

The stigmatization of homeless mothers is intimately
bound up with this false line dividing those in need and those
without it, those who are insufficient and those who are self-
sufficient, those who live in the world dependently and those
who live in it independently. Indeed, the firmness of the line
is sustained in part by the very desire of the more socially
legitimated populations to see themselves in a particular set
of ways. The blurring of these lines—through a much richer
discussion of variable degrees and types of dependency,
interdependency, and assistance, and the elimination of the
false vocabulary of "self-sufficiency"—is a crucial part of
what is needed to endow homeless mothers with greater dignity and to create a more honest experience of connections
between "us" and "them." The problem is that such redescrip-
tions, such revised narratives, will disturb the self-assurance
of powerful constituencies whose identities are fragile. These
constituencies include those who favor assistance for the
poor almost as much as those who oppose it, those who work

in places like WCC, almost as much as those who work in corporate offices.

Consider what these vocabularies, as well as the even harsher vocabularies of the media and antipoor politicians, infuse into the identities of poor women. How does one experience being portrayed as a "welfare queen," a "baby factory," or an "alligator?" Jane, a twenty-seven-year-old mother of two currently taking classes at a community college, explains it this way:

> I just don't feel good. I don't feel proud. I really don't. I used to like going grocery shopping. . . . I was excited to get my little stuff, and now I'm not. I'm embarrassed to use food stamps. You're not treated nicely. . . . I want to go to the checker with the less people. I don't want people behind me. I want them to close off—you know how they close the line when you're in there. I want them to do that. I don't want them there. It's embarrassing.

Jane has internalized larger cultural judgments about her to the point that she is embarrassed to go to the store. She dreads the essential task of buying food and other household goods for her family. She has been made to feel that she does not deserve them: "They think it's all free, that it's all free to you. And they don't treat you nice. They're mean."

Or consider another example of internalized contempt from one of Kingfisher's informants:

> I was living in this one apartment and waiting for [them], you know you wait for food stamps to come . . . and, for like three or four or five days. . . . I hope our food stamps come, and this was when I first moved to Penrose, and was living in kind of a middle class . . . neighborhood. . . . I hated to go outside the door 'cause I felt so different . . . and I went through a whole thing there where I wouldn't even check my mail until after

dark, you know I just felt so odd. . . . anyway, so . . . it was one day, and the mailman came, and Dale [he] was like three or something and he was outside playing, he saw the mailman put the food stamps in the mailbox and he started screaming, "MOM, OUR FOOD STAMPS ARE HERE! MOM OUR FOOD STAMPS ARE HERE!" like this [laughing] and in one way it was really funny, but in another way it was so pathetic . . . you know, and he was waiting so desperately for 'em too . . . you know, and, it was just, and that's how it was. (In Kingfisher 1996, 31–32)

This story is both poignant and revealing in its irony. This woman points not only to how internalized the stigma of assistance can be but also to the intense role that children play in how women negotiate and experience those stigmas. This mother notes how part of what was "humiliating" and pathetic" to her was that her son was also waiting for the food stamps, "desperately" waiting. His excitement shows that food is not something he can take for granted. And his public announcement doubly embarrasses his mother: he proclaims not only their insufficient income but also her inability to provide him with basic needs, a fundamental tenet of good motherhood.

One of the dilemmas in welfare policy is that it attempts to provide families with only a subsistence level of support (actually failing to do even this, according to Edin and Lein 1997; Polakow 1993). However, norms of good motherhood dictate that mothers care for their children above and beyond this level. Indeed, Edin and Lein point out that the single exception to all of the mothers they interviewed, the only woman who did not supplement her welfare benefits with other income, was under investigation by Children's Protective Services for neglect because her child lacked adequate food and clothing (1997, 42).

But being a good mother means allowing children to be

children, and in childhood one is expected to receive treats at least sometimes. At WCC we often addressed the problem of a family's overextending its budget because of a holiday or family birthday. Families want their children to participate in the larger cultural practices of celebration, but bare budgets do not allow for this (Kingfisher 1996; Edin and Lein 1997). One welfare recipient in Edin and Lein's study described this dilemma: "You know, we live in such a materialistic world. Our welfare babies have needs and wants too. They see other kids going to the circus, having toys and stuff like that. You gotta do what you gotta do to make your kid feel normal. There is no way you can deprive your child" (1997, 30).

This, then, is yet another bind. On one hand, in order to be viewed as moral and deserving of benefits, one must correspond with the norms of good motherhood and responsible expenditures. On the other hand, it is often enough necessary to break the norms of responsible expenditure in order to try to live up to the standard of allowing your children to partake in the paradigmatic practices of consumption and celebration in this culture.

At times, these compromises can become sites of resistance. For example, Kingfisher cites a story of a pregnant welfare recipient who spent all of her monthly income to produce a decent Christmas for her children. Kingfisher points out the defiance in this story, the insistence of self-worth. And yet such resistance may itself be so tied to mainstream materialism and social norms of maternal responsibility that its effects remain primarily self-destructive:

> For instance, in recounting her use of rent money for Christmas presents, Susan produces a story of resistance to both welfare regulations and an ideology that says that poor people shouldn't have "luxuries," especially at taxpayers' expense. In her resistance, however, Susan accommodates both

consumerism and the dominant view that it is a parent's (in this case a mother's) responsibility to provide for all a child's needs and wants. (1996, 31)

While clients search for and sometimes find methods of resistance, the patterns of resistance available to them are likely to play into the hands of those who would demonize them. The lack of respect that clients feel in relation to their welfare status is well documented (Gordon 1994; Ehrenreich and Piven 1984; Schein 1995; White 1996; Kingfisher 1996; Edin and Lein 1997; Epstein 1997; Polakow 1993). WCC clients on welfare often described their brusque treatment at welfare offices; errors from the agency frequently threatened people's housing and ability to get by (checks not coming on time or incorrect payments); waits at the welfare offices were always lengthy; and there was a general feeling of suspicion and persecution from welfare workers.

For example, Sandy, a WCC program supervisor, used to work for Adult Family Services (welfare) in California. She described the bureaucratic wall of resistance she hit when she tried to use her own car instead of a state-issued car to make home visits. She explained to her supervisors that a state car parked in the driveway was embarrassing to clients. It virtually announced to the neighborhood their impoverished status. Sandy felt that a small gesture of respect might help clients maintain a sense of pride and dignity. Yet her supervisors refused to acknowledge this as a legitimate concern. They insisted that she use the state car. But, then, workers sometimes resist, too. And Sandy continued to drive her own car.

Such compassion and recognition of a client's sense of self may be more the exception than the rule among welfare workers (Kingfisher 1996). Often enough, welfare workers conform to those rules that help to perpetuate the stigma attached to welfare reliance. Certainly, recipients to some degree internalize this experience of devaluation, even as they often try to fend it off. Let Ruth, a WCC client, summarize:

> I tell people, "Yeah, I'm on welfare and I'm not proud of it. But it's something that keeps a roof over my kids' head, and that's my main goal. . . . It gives them food and it gives them clothes." So I go, "Yes, I do want to get off welfare, and I will." I know I will. . . . That's one of my biggest goals that sits on top. . . . I know a lot of people take advantage of welfare. I think that's why they're doing what they're doing with the welfare system. . . . But about wanting to put kids in orphanages, now that I think is wrong. That's dead wrong because no kid deserves to be in an orphanage. That's just as bad as being in a foster home, and I wouldn't put that on anyone, because I've been there, and it's not fun to be in foster homes. . . .
>
> That's what welfare is . . . just that little extra help to just get you by and let you know that your kids aren't gonna be on the streets or you're not gonna be homeless. . . . It's supposed to help, not jeopardize you if you don't do something right, and now you're gonna be cut off welfare and your kids are going into orphanages or foster homes because that's not good. That's just gonna make things worse. . . . They are gonna have more people out on the street than they do now because even at this minute there are more homeless families than are getting the help that they need. . . . That's just gonna make things worse if you're taking kids away from families that love them. . . . They would have a hell of a time trying to get my kids away from me.

Ruth describes her welfare status both aggressively and defensively, explaining quickly that she has plans to get off the welfare rolls as soon as she can. So in some ways she illustrates a fundamental premise of welfare services: the more uncomfortable recipients are made to feel about their welfare status, the more apt they will be to get off the rolls. Of course,

Ruth has not actually been able to get off welfare—she just wants to.

Ruth also points to the cruelties and hypocrisies in some of the current welfare policies and the potential directions it may head in. She explains that welfare should be fundamentally about help and support, not about jeopardizing families, threatening to tear them apart. She worries about the repercussions of welfare reform because it is based on inadequate understandings of homeless families. She fears she could even lose custody of her children, recognizing that state control can move in many directions that are likely to affect her but over which she will have no control.

While Ruth worries that welfare reforms might threaten the custody of her children, Sally offers an example of how welfare bureaucracy can lead to desperation that threatens to tear families apart. Sally describes when she first arrived in Portland, fleeing a dangerous scenario in another state. She found herself sleeping in a park with her three children, unable to access either food or shelter:

> A lot of shelters would not take me because I have a twelve-year-old son. . . . They says, "Well, is there anybody else [you can turn to]?" And I'm sitting there, "If there was, do you think I'd be calling you?" I says, "So in other words, I've got to shoot my son and get rid of my other kids in order for you to help me?" . . . I was not very nice, because I was just so stressed out. I mean, I used every word in the book, but that's how upset I was.

Sally's situation was further exacerbated by the fact that she was unable to use her food stamps with an out-of-state license. Her sense of overwhelming desperation heightened:

> And I was even thinking at the time . . . "God, what kind of mother am I to put my kids through this?" Mark [her oldest

son] says, "Mom, don't even think about it. Please don't give us up, Mom. Please don't give us up." And he was reading my mind. . . . And of course, Mark got real upset, and I don't blame him 'cause I was going to give them up, and I was gonna kill myself. That's what was on my mind real strong.

Social policies, welfare regulations, and bureaucratic red tape do not just discipline citizens into conformity with cultural norms such as a work ethic and traditional family values. In an effort to keep from making life "too easy" for recipients, "too appealing and desirable," social service limitations and contradictions may push individuals even closer to the edge.

Two-parent families also struggle with cultural norms and ideologies perpetuated through welfare regulations. In a culture where men are supposed to provide economically for their families, failing to do so disrupts masculine identities and further stigmatizes the family as misusing and undeserving of state resources. However, as Michelle points out here, men also experience difficulties trying to care for their families. These dilemmas perhaps need to be understood within their structural contexts rather than serving as points of critique against particular men. Michelle describes their current situation:

Tony [Michelle's boyfriend] is gonna be twenty in August, and he has really no experience of a good job. You can't expect a young father to have everything. I guess I get mad at Tony a lot because he doesn't have a job, but then I look at this situation, and I'm like, wait a minute, Tony has hardly any experience and he was a young father and he was there and he's still here, and that's a big thing to be proud of—that he's still around. 'Cause most fathers, I would have to say, woulda taken off. Especially [given] that he was sixteen. . . . That's young. . . . Even if Tony hasn't been around to pay for everything with Marissa, he has done everything he can. I mean Tony, he's a good person.

Michelle reminds us here that fathers need to be evaluated on more multifaceted fronts than simply their ability to provide financial security. In her case, she and Tony had their first child when they were very young; this has worked against Tony's ability to procure and hold solid employment. Michelle insists that we remember these circumstances when we hold him up to particular cultural standards. And she also reminds us that he has "stayed around" in spite of these hardships. Indeed, perhaps one of the reasons many men would have "taken off" is the humiliation and frustration they feel when struggling to fit social expectations that do not adequately address or reflect their circumstances.

Clients are not the only ones to complain about welfare. WCC staff also gripe about it bitterly. Welfare policies seem to be in a constant state of flux, and it is often impossible to untangle them. The paperwork that welfare workers demand from other social service agencies and clients always seems unnecessarily long, complex, and repetitive. Welfare workers frequently did not return calls to WCC staff or clients, and with some exceptions of course, they seemed to be some of the most disagreeable people set in one of the most muddled and rude environments around. As one WCC supervisor said, "They're [AFS and so forth] supposed to be for the poor but they're not. . . . I mean, everything that they do is almost a contradiction of that."

The WCC program director, Margaret, voiced concerns about the notion that the selective repeal of benefits will get people "off their butts and working":

> In the welfare reform, I think there is a mean-spiritedness. . . .
> I don't hear, "Let's cut out the bureaucracy." I hear, "Let's cut
> out the benefits," . . . because the bureaucrats are unwilling to

look at themselves and name themselves as the problem. I think that maybe 5 percent of the people will "get off their butts" and get a job. Others will find another way to live off someone else in some predatory way, and others will simply suffer. It's my experience that most people who are on welfare hate being on welfare—they find it punitive and humiliating and would get off it if they could. . . . I mean, the system is really faulty, and things like inadequate child care and transportation and all that are truly a problem.

Jack, the housing coordinator, disagrees with our director on this point. He argues that transportation, child care, and health care are merely part of an endless list of excuses used to keep clients on federal funding and to allow them to not work. He believes a stronger work ethic needs to be instilled in families, forcing them to become more self-sufficient. In some ways at least, Jack may exemplify the prototypical disaffected working-class male described by William Connolly (cited earlier). As Jack explains:

We need to start instilling those kinds of things in families. . . . there's no reason you can't get up and get a job. . . . Now you take a mom who hasn't worked, and you put her on at McDonald's, and maybe you do pay for her child care for a little bit, but I think it's a limited time that you give that person. You have to give that only to get going. . . . I think people perform under that pressure [of] . . . "I can't keep paying your child care indefinitely." [Without that pressure] people jump up and quit jobs when they were doing fine, [saying], . . . "I didn't like my boss," or "I don't like the people I work with." Well shit, I don't like my boss sometimes, or I don't like the people that I work with, but also I gotta pay my rent. So I didn't just up and quit. I made sure I had something else in place. . . . I didn't just up and decide to move from Colorado to [another state], so now I'm homeless and I've got no fu-

ture. I'm amazed at people who do that. . . . I'm thinking,
"How could you do that?"

Jack admits that he has not always had it easy. And that encourages him to think that welfare "makes it easy" for welfare
recipients. It is difficult for him to think that there may be
two constituencies who have it hard in two related but different ways.

Jack understands capitalism and the social stratification it
engenders as necessary and positive. He criticizes those who
argue against work proposals in welfare reform, suggesting
that the model of "moving up the ladder" is a good thing, as
well as desiring public acceptance that people are going to
have different standards of living:

> Some people say, "Well, the only jobs out there are entry-level
> jobs at McDonald's." Well, geez, I hope you're not planning
> on staying at McDonald's your whole life. . . . [But] if what it
> takes to get started is french fries, then maybe you work your
> way up to [the] register and then maybe work your way up to
> assistant manager, or quit McDonald's and go over to the car
> wash as an assistant manager. I want people to have dreams
> like that. . . . [Otherwise,] we'd have to do away with all the
> available jobs. We'd have no McDonald's, because there'd be
> nobody to cook the burgers 'cause nobody would wanna do it.

Jack feels the current welfare system makes it too easy for individuals not to work. He suggests that this promotes their
desire to live off the system. Jack too feels we shouldn't feed
the alligators—at least not very much or for very long.

There is a huge distance between Jane, a WCC client, and
Jack, even while you can hear common glimmers between
their experiences. Jane expresses her aversion to welfare,
which she has been on sporadically since she had her first
baby at age sixteen: "I never wanted to be on it to begin with.

I swore I would never, ever, ever have a baby and be on welfare. And here I am. I never wanted to do that. And then I had another baby and got on welfare again."

Jack would blame Jane for her own predicament, perhaps citing the irresponsibility of having a baby before she could finance her care independently. Jane voices some anger at herself, too, for ending up on welfare when she promised herself she never would. But she also articulates a strong critique of the system and portions some of the blame outside of herself:

> The system's set up now so that you can't have a family in order to get help. . . . At AFDC you can't have the baby's father with you in order to get help, so they are basically encouraging fathers to leave their children even while they are telling fathers to stay with their children. . . . And most places you can't get into a shelter with a man. The ones that I had to go to, John [her boyfriend] and I had to separate in order for us to get any kind of shelter. And then he just kinda had to do his own thing, and even if he was clean, the only place he knew where to go was where they were using drugs, in order to not be outside at night.

Jane points here to the kinds of hypocrisies that the current welfare system creates, complicating her life in unnecessary ways, while Jack's sympathies are controlled by the model of individual responsibility through which he gains meaning in his life. It would take a lot of work to promote more positive lines of communication between these two perspectives.

The current welfare system is designed to set up individuals for failure. It promotes resentment and animosity between workers and clients, produces stigmatized public identities of clients, and fosters internal and external disrespect of clients. Thus, rather than offering a genuine means of alleviating poverty, welfare is mired in a politics of blame and a maintenance of social stratification.

I do not pretend to have offered a complete view of welfare here. Indeed, welfare is not the central subject of my inquiry. However, one would be hard pressed to examine poverty and homelessness in the United States without addressing the welfare system. As we have seen, the kinds of policies and representations that affect the welfare state today provide a discursive frame in which WCC staff and clients participate to different degrees as they make sense of the poverty and dilemmas they face.

The individualization of blame inherent in the welfare system is apparent in all corollary social services as well. From drug addiction programs, to homeless services, to teen parenting programs, to psychotherapy, the common premise is that it is the individual who is deficient and needs fixing. Even in the face of WCC's burgeoning alternative model of strength-based service, the premise of the self-contained individual is maintained. Whether the focus is on the potential or the lack of the individual, the individual is the subject that remains constant. Social services are caught between enacting a set of strategies that absolve the larger political economy of responsibility for homelessness by placing the burden on the individual, and trying to challenge that single-minded conception in ways that threaten to dry up the limited resources now available to them. Until this contradiction is softened, we will continue to have a system of assistance that threatens to break down under its own weightlessness.

6. Leaving the Field

After a year and a half of living in Portland, it was time to return to California. It was hard to tell people at WCC that I was leaving. I felt like I was letting them down, dropping the ball, adding to their already overburdened workloads. In some ways I already felt the familiar signs of social work burnout. In other ways, I had just settled into my groove, having established a set of competencies as a social service provider.

I was not sure what I was going back to. California did not feel like home. Graduate school felt a million miles away.

I continued to keep up my field journals, but it felt less pressing than it had at the beginning. Work was work; the need for interpretation was less clear. I wrote in my field journal:

> It feels like there hasn't been that much going on at work. I think that's true to a certain degree, but it's also become so normal to me that it's hard to see it anymore. It's hard to muster up the enthusiasm to write about it. There's no longer

any novelty. Besides, it's impossible to imagine ever being so distant that I would need notes to jog my memory.

The agency was in a state of upheaval as I prepared to depart. Job descriptions were being redefined; some people had been laid off, and many others were being relocated within the agency. I began to question the foundation of the agency itself and wondered if the executive decisions being made were truly for the best. Morale was low, staff turnover was high.

The last family to come on my caseload was full of complications. They had driven here from out of state, following that familiar desire to make a new start in a place where they had no connections. This was an extended family. The mother's name was Carolyn. She was an African American woman in her late thirties. Her three children were with her—a sixteen-year-old daughter, an eighteen-year-old son, and a twenty-year-old son named Matt. Matt had a nineteen-year-old girlfriend named Grace, and together they had a one-year-old son, Kenyon. Additionally, Carolyn's sixteen-month-old niece, Sarah, was with them, although it was never clear exactly why.

Carolyn was very articulate and appeared to be highly motivated. She said she had already found temporary employment and an apartment. The apartment was not available for about a week, and so they needed temporary shelter. The case looked as though it might be clear-cut and short-term.

Grace approached me that first afternoon in the day shelter while I was going over paperwork with Carolyn. She had been sitting a little bit away from us, and I had felt her watching the interactions. Perhaps she was feeling alienated from our discussions or was sizing me up, or both. Grace is an attractive Latina woman with anxious mannerisms and the tendency to talk fast. Matt was on the couch with their young son lying on top of him taking a nap. He had barely acknowledged me and showed no plans of ever doing so.

Grace sat down at the table next to me, her white T-shirt torn and a little smeared. She said that the only reason she was with the family was that she and Matt had not been able to resolve custody debates over Kenyon. She said that they were having trouble in their relationship and that both wanted custody. Carolyn looked uncomfortable and Matt seemed nonchalant, although I sensed he was listening as Grace poured all this out to me. I sat quietly and let her talk. Grace said she had a felony conviction in Arizona and that she had jumped probation some time ago. She asked if I could help get her name cleared because she felt like a fugitive. I said we could meet the next day to discuss it further. I also suggested that she and Matt set up an appointment with our mediation specialist to reach some agreements about their relationship and their respective places in Kenyon's life. Grace nodded enthusiastically, but Matt replied negatively: "Things are not *that* bad," he said curtly, without looking at me. "Everything will be fine once we move into our new place." I let it go at that for the day.

When I met Grace alone the next day, she shared more of her story. Her parents divorced when she was young. She lived for several years with her mother, whom she described as physically and emotionally abusive. During these years Grace was also sexually abused by a boyfriend of her mother's, a family friend, and an uncle. Then, when Grace was twelve years old, her mother moved with her boyfriend to another state, leaving Grace alone. So she has been on her own since she was twelve. Grace's half brother was taken in by their maternal grandmother, but she refused to take Grace because she is "Mexican" (her father is Mexican, her mother white). The courts put Grace in her father's custody based on her mother's "abandonment."

Grace's father was an alcoholic and a crack addict. She said he did nothing to take care of her—neither providing basic clothing or food nor enrolling her in school. Grace had to fight the school principal to enroll herself. She won that struggle because, as she said to me, "I have a right to an education." Grace wanted the state to take custody of her and said she would have preferred living in foster homes. However, every time she moved in with a foster family, her father would sabotage the arrangement by showing up drunk or high and making a scene, fighting with the foster family until they were unwilling to keep Grace.

Eventually, Grace started staying with various friends and tried to maintain as much distance from her father as possible. She was supposed to receive child support checks from the state because her father was on disability, but she didn't learn about them until she was sixteen. Then, when she tried to get some of the money from her father, he gave her the "runaround." When Grace was a sophomore in high school, she got pregnant:

> I was really scared. I didn't think I was ready for a baby. I still acted really, like, on the spur of the moment all the time. . . . And I didn't know if I could give him everything he was gonna need—you know, give him the right kind of life. Plus, I didn't know if I was gonna be with him the way my mom was with me—abusive and all that. So I gave him, James, up for adoption. I thought giving my baby up was going to be the hardest decision I would ever have to make. But things keep right on being hard.

A year or so later, when Grace was seventeen, she was mugged by four men and beaten up. She felt angry, scared, and confused. She bought a gun. Four days later she and a girlfriend were driving around looking for the perpetrators so she could retaliate. She said she wanted to "do something,"

but she wasn't sure what. They did not find the assailants.
Instead, they pulled into a convenience store:

> I told Joleena that I was going to rob the place. She didn't
> think I was serious. I was so angry, just pumped. I kept flash-
> ing on the faces of those guys who jumped me. I kept seeing
> them. Joleena just sat in the car while I went inside. I robbed
> them and then came running out screaming, "Drive!" to
> Joleena, who was just sitting there.

Grace and Joleena drove away, but they were picked up half
an hour later by the police. Grace was charged with armed
robbery (she had taken the loaded gun in with her). She was
put in jail pending her court date. Her paternal grandmother
gave her father money to get Grace out on bail. Grace's father
used the money on himself, for crack she believes, and then
came and visited her in jail empty-handed. He never mentioned that he had been able to get her out. Instead, he told
her that he was sorry he could not help her.

Grace was sentenced to community service and probation
and was released. At first, Grace said, she was responsible
about maintaining her legal commitments. Then Grace met
Matt, and they started dating. Two months after the relationship began, Grace became pregnant. Matt convinced Grace to
move out of state with him. He said he wanted them to make
a fresh start. So Grace "jumped" probation, and they moved
to Illinois. During her pregnancy Matt and Grace's relationship deteriorated:

> Everything was different. I didn't have any friends or any-
> thing. I wanted to break up with him, but whenever I tried,
> he'd tell me he was gonna turn me in to the police and that I'd
> have my baby behind bars. He said that then he would take
> the baby from me while I was still in jail and I would never
> see him. I felt like a prisoner anyway. Matt wouldn't let me

go anywhere. I ate all the time. When I met Matt, I weighed 130 pounds—then I got up to 175. When I had nothing to do, I would just feed my face even though I wasn't hungry. If I couldn't think of anything to do—I'd just think of something to cook!

Grace pulled a picture out of her wallet and showed it to me. She looked much heavier in it, with a worse complexion and greasy lifeless hair pulled back into a ponytail. She had lost most of the weight she had gained and looked healthier now.

Grace gave birth to Kenyon while she and Matt were living in Illinois. She was unhappy with her living arrangements but was too scared to return to Arizona. The robbery had been highly publicized on television in her small town, and she was certain that she would be discovered and punished for jumping probation. Grace was terrified of losing custody of Kenyon and of going to jail. Matt told her if she went back to jail, he would never allow her to see Kenyon again. So she lived in fear of the law. She shortened her name from Graciella to Grace and changed her last name from her biological father's name, Mendoza, to her stepfather's, Lawson.

Her relationship with Matt continued to worsen. He constantly called her a "bitch" and slapped her in ways he called "playful" but that upset and hurt her. He held the power of turning her in as his ultimate card. He also punched her hard while she was holding Kenyon, leaving a bruise that lasted for six months. They fought constantly and disagreed about parenting strategies. He said that she spoiled their son. He used spanking and time-outs as disciplinary techniques. Grace felt that he should not spank so hard or so often. It was hard for me to imagine that either tactic was appropriate for a child barely one year old.

Grace pleaded with Matt for a separation. She said she wanted to share custody, even trading off every other night if he wanted. Matt refused, telling her it had to be "all or noth-ing." When Matt's family decided to move to the Northwest, he wanted to go with them. Grace felt uncomfortable around his mother, saying that even though she had always treated Carolyn with great respect, she always felt ostracized by her. Carolyn sometimes grew enraged over Grace and Matt's rela-tionship, one time saying to her son, "Look what you brought into my house!" which Grace believed referred to her crimi-nal background as well as her ethnicity. In spite of her hesi-tancy, Grace felt that Matt held all the cards, so she came with them.

By now over a week had passed, and I was working only minimally with the rest of the family. Carolyn had stopped contacting me after she received her motel voucher. The family soon moved into their new apartment, and Grace said Carolyn was working full time. Her other teenage son was also working, and I had given Matt some employment refer-rals, though he never followed through on them. My energy was focused on Grace.

Grace, above all, wanted to leave Matt. She wanted to clear her name and to return to Arizona with her son. I began work-ing to get her a lawyer, not an easy process in my line of work. Legal Aid will only take the most straightforward cases and will have nothing to do with criminal charges. Even these mini-mal services are being defunded as part of federal cutbacks on services for the poor. Finally, through a low-income lawyer-referral service, I found a lawyer who set fees on a sliding scale. It still was going to cost $50 just for an initial consultation.

Grace and I met with the lawyer, an informal young woman who listened intently and respectfully to Grace's story and then agreed to do the case for free, dropping even the initial fee. She said she would try to get the charges against Grace dropped over the phone, and that she thought she could suc-ceed without much trouble.

Unfortunately, things were not as easy as she had hoped. The district attorney in Arizona said that there was a fugitive warrant out for Grace's arrest and that while the police were not looking for her actively, if she got picked up for anything (e.g., speeding or jaywalking), she would be flown back to Arizona under armed guard to serve jail time. The minimum sentence she could receive was ten years. However, they could give her as many as twenty-five years. And the DA warned that they might give her the higher sentence, especially if they had to go to all the trouble of extraditing her.

Grace's only other option was to return to Arizona and turn herself in. The lawyer said the DA seemed like a reasonable guy, and she thought he would recommend no jail time and just reinstate her probation. However, there was no guarantee. He could also decide that she had had her chance, was no longer under eighteen, and deserved jail time. The DA also informed her lawyer that Matt had already attempted to turn Grace in twice, once from Illinois and once from here, letting them know her whereabouts and her name change.

I shared this grim news with Grace at a smoky diner near her apartment. She showed her courage. She said she could not keep running, and she just had to go and deal with it. I agreed to help her return to Arizona.

After considering several options with my director, Margaret, we decided that the only reasonable way to get Grace to Arizona was by plane. If we sent her by bus, it was possible that Matt would figure out the bus route and intercept. And if we sent her on an indirect route, he might beat her there and endanger her at the other end. So I managed to finagle a decently priced ticket that we bought with client assistance money. Grace was scheduled to fly out three days later, the same morning I was leaving Portland for California.

The next question was where she was going to stay once she arrived. I used a national domestic violence directory to locate the shelter nearest to her hometown. They said they would not help her because of her criminal background. I became enraged at them and eventually wrote them a scathing letter. The categorical repudiation of clients with a criminal history rules out too many people who need assistance. In particular, prostitutes are often denied domestic violence services because of their so-called criminal backgrounds. To deny these women services undermines any possibility of antiviolence work. Domestic violence needs to be addressed in all the contexts in which it occurs. Those contexts are often ugly and complicated and include run-ins with the law.

Eventually, I found a homeless shelter that could accommodate Grace when she and Kenyon arrived. Her legal history and the possibility of family complications if Matt followed her were things they felt able to handle. I was concerned that it would not be as safe as a domestic violence shelter but was grateful for their help. Certainly, WCC could never promise services to anyone from out of town when they arrived. But I was also nervous for Grace. The shelter sounded larger and more anonymous than anything we participated in.

I gave Grace the information and told her to call them when she arrived. "Will there be someone there like you?" she asked me nervously as we sat in my car—having finally finished all the errands we had to do to prepare for her departure. Rain poured down on the windshield. Kenyon had fallen asleep in the car seat in the back. Grace searched my eyes anxiously. "No one has ever really helped me before."

"I'm sure there will be great people there," I assured her. "You will just have to look into services when you get there."

"I'm just not sure the plan is *safe* enough" she told me. I smiled inside, thinking about how I was always stressing the importance of safety to her, and now she was tossing that language back to me.

"What can we do to make it safer?" I asked.

"Nothing," she replied solemnly.

Then, after a pause she asked me, "So, are you nervous about leaving?"

"I guess I am," I admitted, flashing for a moment on my pending move.

"Me, too," she said. "I guess I better get back before Matt starts to wonder where I am." I helped her unload Kenyon from my car and hugged her good-bye as she held him.

"You take care of yourself, now. You stay safe," I instructed her, just to have something to say.

"You, too," she answered. "And don't worry—everything will work out for you. You are one of those people that things fall in place for." I wished I could have said the same to her. Instead, I quietly watched her hoist her bag onto her shoulder, adjust Kenyon's weight, and walk away.

The next day was the day of departures. I had wanted to drive Grace to the airport that morning before I drove out of town. Her flight was at 7:00 A.M., and I wanted to know that she got there. But Margaret had refused that plan, saying it was too dangerous. And in that way she enforced stronger boundaries between me and Grace, boundaries that she worried were becoming too porous, especially given my own vulnerabilities at the time. I had become identified with Grace's predicament in a way that I now think was both dangerous and essential, at least to some degree, to the job itself. But Margaret had been in the field long enough to know when you also need to set limits to such inevitable identifications. She allocated client money for a cab instead. She was right, as usual.

Grace missed her flight. Matt and his mother had an all-night brawl the previous night. Grace wasn't able to slip away in the early morning hours because everyone was still awake. Finally, around 11:00 A.M. she slipped out for a walk with Kenyon. All she had was a diaper bag and one change of clothes. She caught a cab to the airport and was able to make a late afternoon flight. She feared what would happen at the other end, and she also felt guilty and scared about leaving Matt and taking Kenyon. She called him just before she boarded the plane. She told him she was leaving. Instead of yelling at her, he was sweet, trying to convince her to stay and work things out. She wavered. She got on the plane.

Once in Arizona she returned to court, and the judge reinstated her probation without jail time. She was relieved and sorry she had not done it earlier. She contacted her half brother and reestablished her relationship with him. He was being very supportive, she told me when I called her from California to make sure she had made it all right. She was going to stay with him for a little while until she found a place. I told her I was also living with my brother until I figured out what I was going to do next. She laughed as we said good-bye for the last time. "Isn't that strange?" she remarked.

Grace's convoluted and distressing circumstances were often on the verge of overwhelming both her and those who tried to help her. At one point, Margaret, who was helping me handle this case, became exasperated. She threw up her hands and said, "You know I really feel myself getting angry at Grace. I just want to say to her that this is too hard for us, and just give it back to her to deal with!" Such an expression of frustration from Margaret was virtually unheard of. She always seemed to have some new approach, some overlooked possibility, some window to open. But even Margaret has her moments when there just doesn't seem to be anything left to do.

Grace's story, like so many stories before hers, is complicated. Because she does not fit into social service categories easily, it is hard to find "services" for her. A need for housing, an abusive and threatening partner, a young child, a police record in another state, and the absence of a social service agency equipped to respond to this complex combination become layered into each other. One of them creates a new obstacle to extrication—just when you think you have surmounted several others. If one has more than a single need, service providers are often at a loss. But individual lives are seldom singular and straightforward. Very often, they are chaotic and cluttered.

The social service approach of today originates from a charity model. That may be one of its pitfalls. The charity model is organized around helping those who are "down on their luck" and who need a quick fix to tide them over until better times. This model assumes that beyond one particular circumstance (e.g., death, illness, natural disaster, joblessness, homelessness) the individual has other personal resources to be "self-sufficient." Not only is the charity model insufficient to the issues facing many poor people today, but its failures operate to foster public pressure to dismantle the welfare state.

While it is crucial to evaluate social assistance programs critically, to consider their limitations or failings without coming up with something else does not speak to the needs of homeless families. In the United States today many people are turning away from an ethic of charity while refusing to pursue any other ethic appropriate to the circumstances and needs of homeless families. This combination fosters a cynicism that might better be replaced by a revised model of social assistance. In a time when many people believe that the homeless are responsible for their own dependencies, those most in need are automatically placed under suspicion.

One of the protections that cynicism offers us is the comfort of distance. It distances us from *identification* with the conditions of those in need, thereby encouraging us to pawn off on them any vulnerabilities we might feel. The most moving thing about working with Grace was my growing realization of the

points of contact between us across significant lines of difference. Grace and I were both leaving relationships; we were
both trying to return to places where we weren't sure what we
would find; and we were both trying to negotiate a series of
details, trials, interruptions, and surprises that had emerged in
our lives. I do not want to deny the key differences in social
class, income, family support, physical safety, socially legitimate work pursuits, and so forth—differences that Grace
summed up when she assured me, "Don't worry.... You are
one of those people that things fall in place for." I do, however,
think that an ethic of care can only overtake the attitude of
cynical distance when we allow ourselves to notice the points
of contact despite multiple differences.

Valerie Polakow provides an example of this when she describes her recognition of the thin but significant line between
herself and the impoverished mothers she was researching:

> I have been profoundly affected by the experience of research-
> ing and writing this book, realizing how little existential dis-
> tance separates my life as a mother from that of the mothers
> and children whose lives are chronicled here. Yet the geogra-
> phy of privilege in the first America puts one in a world apart
> from the grim contingency of life on the edges in the other
> America. (1993, 3)

Such a terrain of stratification distances us not only from
identifications but also from the assumptions of implication
in the lives of those who have fallen through the porous social
nets of employment, family support, and education. The
charity model, then, is not all bad. Its ethic of care needs to be
reworked in new circumstances of poverty and homelessness.
The primacy of the charity model and the resulting cynicism
created by its failure encourage a politics in which the privileged give themselves too much credit for their achievements
by bestowing too much blame on the down-and-out for their

conditions. This last form of distance may provide the most psychic and cultural protection of all. It obscures from us how overwhelming things would seem to us, too, if we were caught in similar circumstances, and it loads 99 percent of the responsibility for failure on those caught in overwhelming situations. But if social workers all too readily become overwhelmed in trying to assist homeless mothers, perhaps we should take that as a sign of how impressive the obstacles are that these mothers have to cope with on a regular basis. Such a response is admittedly difficult to marshal, for it would scramble the very culture of cynicism through which so many protect themselves from the gaze of the down-and-out.

I have engaged chapters in the lives of particular women in ways that stay close to their experiences while setting up roadblocks to cynical interpretations of those lives. I have tried to investigate dynamics and relationships from an "on-the-ground" position. I question the omnipotent, all-seeing "god trick," as Donna Haraway puts it, understanding my work to be particularly situated and ethically invested (1991).

I do not imagine that my explorations of intricate, variable, and sometimes elusive relations do or could enable me to uncover all the power relations implicated here. Nor do I imagine that my responses to the power relations I do examine will remain entirely insulated from some of the very critiques I offer against others. But by engaging these relations, and by becoming sensitive to both modes of suffering and to hidden possibilities and limitations within naturalized practices, one might contribute to that diffuse project of freedom that animates much of critical anthropology and feminism. Not freedom from power, but freedom as the provision of new spaces of empowerment for those whose hurts and injuries are obscured, devalued, or defined as necessary by existing regimes of power (Foucault 1979).

One advantage of ethnography is that it allows you to call

into question both vilified and sanitized representations of marginal women. My ethnographic explorations traverse the intersection of cultural norms and individual lives, attempting to illuminate each as a means of shining light on the other. Such an ethnographic project, however, has its dangers. There are constituencies, particularly in this conservative era, that will frame these stories only in the vocabulary of blame, castigation, and punishment.

Anthropologist Laura Nader underlined this risk in the early 1970s when she wrote: "Don't study the poor and powerless because everything you say will be used against them" (1972). Such a caution must be taken into consideration when writing about marginalized populations. However, to refuse to give voice to marginalized women is to render the complexity of their lives invisible. It is to become complicit in their stigmatization. So I have attempted to walk the tightrope of describing the pain, ugliness, and cruelty that often enters into these lives as well as the tenacity and heroism that sometimes emerges as they struggle against the odds they face.

Phillipe Bourgois, in his ethnographic account of crack dealers in El Barrio, articulates the problem:

> Countering traditional moralistic biases and middle class hostility toward the poor should not come at the cost of sanitizing the suffering and destruction that exists on inner city streets. Out of a righteous, or a "politically sensitive," fear of giving the poor a bad image, I refuse to ignore or minimize the social misery I witnessed, because that would make me complicitous with oppressions. (1995, 12)

Bourgois points to a dilemma I share. In an era of punitive characterizations and policies toward the down-and-out, sanitized presentations of their lives mostly open the door for others to represent the ugly stuff in the worst possible light. Sure, the ugly stuff threatens to become drawn back into those crude cultural simplifications. But sometimes it might be possible to break out of this bind: close attention to the complexity and ambiguity of concrete lives might enable us to challenge the adequacy of either of these responses. Perhaps such close attention will show how formulaic those stark contrasts are that divide individuals into absolute categories: deserving/undeserving, innocent/guilty, good/bad, independent/dependent. It may suggest how policies that offer genuine opportunities while allowing for self-esteem, personal growth, and empowerment can create more productive results than the punitive and regulatory ones currently in vogue.

While there may be useful generalizations to be gleaned from this study, they are more likely to be general maxims of the sort that take into account the long-term disruptive effects that accidents, mistakes, bursts of passion, unexpected demands, and so on can have on women in marginal situations. My goal has not been to represent a microcosmic version of homeless families in the larger culture, precisely because I do not believe that such a reflection is possible. In this study, "homeless mothers" do sometimes emerge as a "type," but the type is understood first and foremost as a cultural production shaped by the negative marks placed by the larger culture on mothers without homes. When I use the phrase *homeless mothers* in a positive sense, it is only after the practice of careful listening and close description has helped me open up lines of distinction within the type itself.

Research that is particularly situated and locally invested must be linked to analyses of hegemonic cultural representations in order to encourage long-range reevaluations of public identities. While theory supports practice and practice refines theory, the two also exist in perpetual tension. Theoretical explorations of identity, for example, often function to disrupt and denaturalize culturally entrenched meanings and self-definitions. Such theories can show how cultural identities are constructed, how they are embodied and resisted by those to whom they are applied, and where it might be productive to shift the terms of cultural constitution. But while such projects form a precondition of cultural change, their immediate relevance for, say, a poor mother fleeing both the police and domestic violence, is minimal. Policy-oriented research may provide more immediate resources. But because such research is silently constrained by the existing structure of social service agencies and political tolerance, applied research often consolidates the very representations that need to be reconfigured (Rhodes 1990).

This tension between theory and policy resides at the center of my work. I try to use it as a productive force—even as I experience it as a challenge that threatens to overwhelm. But I cannot end with my own words and goals. For the women I have worked with intimate more effectively the kinds of hopes that sustain them. I neither dismiss these hopes as little more than thinly disguised misery nor embrace them as final visions of a more satisfying world. I offer them, rather, as a testimony to the strength and tenacity of many women living in difficult circumstances.

Ruth summoned this thought about her future goals, just before she was to move into public housing:

> After we get settled, I'm gonna start my schooling. That's one of my main goals . . . to get a better education with computers and stuff. Where I can get a better job so I won't have to be on welfare. One of my goals is getting off welfare. . . . Mainly, it's all for my kids . . . because I want them to have a better life. I want them to have the greatest life that they ever possibly can have. . . . My dream is for my kids to just get to be kids, so they don't have to feel like they're grown up already. . . . Our goal is

happiness because we deserve it. And when we get this place, I think from here out it's just gonna be good. Well, we might have a few bumpy roads but . . . it's gonna be smooth sailing, and it's gonna be great!

Michelle concludes with a dream:

I've always wanted to go to Africa . . . in the jungle part. Just to kind of see what it's like. Monkeys are my favorite animal. . . . I guess I kind of want to be another Jane Goodall. She was just a wonderful person. I mean, the way she was actually able to interact with the chimpanzees and gorillas was amazing. . . . Someday I'll be like that though, Debbie. Someday I'll be famous, and I'll have a monkey on my shoulder.

Hannah looks toward the future this way:

I want to go to . . . school in college for a while . . . as soon as I figure out which way I want to go. I've been finding out a lot of things that I wouldn't mind doing like fish and wildlife. . . . It seems like that's the kind of stuff I want to do 'cause it deals with animals and everything, it deals with outdoors up in the hills—where there's no traffic.

Melanie hopes for this:

I just want to get my life together . . . and to focus on myself and my kids. Then I think things will be a lot better. Also, I think if I stay out of relationships, I mean not completely, but if I don't make them number one in my life—or even number two . . . 'cause I have too much to deal with already, and dealing with a relationship is even more. It's too much. . . . For work—I'm not really sure what I want to do. I need to look at that more.

And Kelly explains:

I just want a home for my kids to feel stable and safe. Angela has never been stable ever. . . . I just want to be really safe.

Terry looks at her past and her future:

> There haven't really been many good times, you know. I re-member the first time I heard Braley laugh. Braley hadn't laughed in months. I heard him laugh, you know, and things are starting to get good. Things are starting to look good. We're homeless and it's hard, but things are still good. I don't know about this. I'm kinda wary . . . but I've always told my-self that what doesn't kill me will make me stronger. There's a reason for everything that has happened. And it's not that bad. It's just a lot of pain. If I could just get back to the origi-nal things, I could probably stop this. You know, if I could deal with those original issues. But I keep getting wrapped up in all this new stuff, and it's not new—it's old. It's all old. It's all the same things. I just gotta get back to the original shit and find a way to deal with it. I don't know. So that's it.

And Sally offers a timely thought:

> It just takes time. You can't judge a person by their past. Not if they're willing to make a change for the better. You gotta give that person a chance.

Notes

Introduction

1. In order to protect the anonymity of those involved, I have changed the names of all the people mentioned here and of the agency where this research took place.

2. According to the 1990 government census the total population of Portland is 424,834 persons. Portland's population is approximately 85 percent white, 7 percent Black, 5 percent Asian or Pacific Islander, 2 percent Native American, Eskimo, or Aleut, and 1 percent other.

3. When I approached the agency, I explained my corresponding research agenda and was granted permission to pursue it. In accordance with human subjects codes, individuals who worked with me on this project and who are represented here were given further explanations of its nature and were asked to sign written consent forms.

1. Kristy

1. WCC makes three types of housing available to clients: motels, church shelters, and transitional housing units. The first two

types can usually be used by a family for up to a month; transitional housing is subsidized for up to three months. But not all of these arrangements are always available, and they are never guaranteed as part of services.

Typically, the staff prefers to put families into one of the family church shelters first and then if necessary the agency puts them up in a motel where they can stay for another month. Thus it was somewhat unusual that Kristy was vouchered into a motel first. This happened because the church shelters were already full when she entered the program. The staff prefers to use the shelter for new clients for several reasons. First, it is free and WCC has a very tight budget. Second, because the agency contracts with two church organizations that run shelters for our families, the agency is expected to keep them at full occupancy when they are open. Third, it seems that some families come to the program because they have heard they can get motel vouchers here and that is all they want. They are not interested in working on other issues or developing a case plan. These families tend to disappear when the voucher is up; they are thus considered a drain on resources that could be reserved for those who might develop a more permanent plan. To give such a family a motel voucher, according to staff philosophy, is to "enable" the behavior that produces and perpetuates homelessness. Offering families a church shelter, replete with supervision, rules, and curfews, "weeds out" families who are looking for a "free ride."

Furthermore, because families in the shelters have to leave them early each morning and not return until dinner, these families often spend the days in our day shelter. This means that staff get to know them quickly and intensely, and issues and concerns often come to the surface more rapidly. Finally, families tend to have a harder time moving from the relative autonomy of the motel to the more structured and supervised living arrangements in the church shelter, and so it is easier if they start out at the shelter.

2. Motherly Things

1. For further discussion of idealized portrayals of family life and corresponding repercussions on contemporary families in the United States, see Coontz (1992).

2. Only 16 percent of the families I worked with at WCC had a biological father present in the family. This picture mirrors the national situation, in which the overwhelming majority of homeless families are headed by single mothers (Homes for the Homeless 1998).

3. Giving the "gift of life" is a notion about maternity and reproduction that has been used in a variety of ideologies. Rickie Solinger in *Wake Up Little Susie: Single Pregnancy and Race before Roe v. Wade* (1992) discusses how between 1945 and 1965 white teens were indoctrinated into the idea that they did not have the right to their illegitimate children. Social services, in alignment with wider cultural ideologies, pressured them to believe that they wanted to give up their children in retribution for their "mistake" of getting pregnant. In return, supposedly, these girls get the "gift" of a second chance at normal middle-class life. Furthermore, antiabortion activists have dramatized the "miracle of life," effectively casting women as having the responsibility to provide this gift to their unborn fetuses.

More currently, Helena Ragoné, in *Surrogate Motherhood: Conception in the Heart* (1994), discusses the cultural narrative propagated by agencies and internalized by surrogate mothers of choosing to devote themselves to bearing a child for a couple as an ultimate act of gift giving.

4. Luker emphasizes that adoption rates have gone down significantly in the past forty years. She notes that from 1965 to 1972, 20 percent of all white babies and 2 percent of all Black babies were given up for adoption. However, from 1982 to 1988 the figures were 3 percent and 1 percent, respectively.

5. For more detailed accounts of abuses such as forced sterilization and their impacts on particular communities, see *Women, Race*

and Class by Angela Davis (1983); *Women under Attack: Victories, Backlash, and the Fight for Reproductive Freedom* edited by Susan Davis (1988); Dorothy Robert's essay "Punishing Drug Addicts Who Have Babies: Women of Color, Equality, and the Right to Privacy" (1991); and several essays in *Mothering: Ideology, Experience, and Agency* (notably those by Evelyn Nakano Glenn, Patricia Hill Collins, and Rickie Solinger), edited by Evelyn Nakano Glenn et al. (1994).

For contemporary discussions about legislation designed to regulate women's childbearing by such means as mandating the implant of the contraceptive Norplant, see Hartouni 1997 (105).

3. Precarious Lives

1. A transitional unit is furnished housing that WCC provides for some clients. It is an apartment (varying in size and location) where clients can live rent free for up to three months. This enables them to save money and to have a place to live while they seek permanent housing.

2. For similar studies and findings, see also Roberts (1991).

3. For further analysis of the false distinction between independent and dependent individuals, see both Coontz (1992) and Fraser and Gordon (1994).

4. In *States of Injury: Power and Freedom in Late Modernity* Brown explores politicized identity and the problem of a liberal conception of the "will": "Revenge as a 'reaction,' a substitute for the capacity to act, produces identity as both bound to the history that produced it and as a reproach to the present which embodies that history. That will that 'took to hurting' in its own impotence against its past becomes (in the form of an identity whose very existence is due to heightened consciousness of the immovability of its 'it was,' its history of subordination) a will that makes not only a psychological but a political practice of revenge, a practice that reiterates the existence of an identity whose present past is one of insistently, unredeemable injury. This past cannot be redeemed *unless* the

identity ceases to be invested in it, and it cannot cease to be invested in it without giving up its identity as such, thus giving up its economy of avenging and at the same time perpetuating its hurt—'when he then stills the pain of the wound *he at the same time infects the wound*'" (73). This issue will return in a more fundamental way when we explore wounded attachments to an ideal of family life that cannot be actualized.

5. Several books have recently been published that analyze women and crack-cocaine addiction. See Humphries (1999), Murphy and Rosenbaum (1999), and Sterk (1999). Given the timing of their release and this book's publication schedule, I am unable to do more than simply point them out as excellent resources on this subject.

6. Ruth's description of being under endless surveillance is reminiscent of Michel Foucault's discussion in *Discipline and Punish* (1979) of Bentham's panopticon. Foucault discusses the way in which prisoners are regulated by the constant potential for surveillance. Ruth describes a similar sense of regulation and punishment; she felt so much resentment and frustration that she hid herself against the watchful eye with a mat and broke one of the cameras.

4. "Patches on the Wound"

1. A case plan is a social service tool whereby a set of goals is established by the client and the worker. These goals are typically laid out in steps that the client must follow in order to obtain self-sufficiency.

5. "Don't Feed the Alligators"

1. Throughout this work when I refer to *welfare*, I am using the term as it is most commonly understood in mainstream politics. Thus, I refer to the federal entitlement programs targeting poor, able-bodied U.S. citizens. These include Adult Family Services (AFS),

Aid to Families with Dependent Children (AFDC), food stamps, and Medicaid.

2. For more in-depth histories of welfare in America, see Gordon (1994) and Skocpol (1992). For a brief but excellent glimpse into welfare reform and history, see White (1996).

Bibliography

Appell, Annette R. 1998. "On Fixing 'Bad' Mothers and Saving Their Children." In *"Bad" Mothers: The Politics of Blame in Twentieth Century America,* ed. Molly Ladd-Taylor and Lauri Umansky. New York: New York University Press.

Badinter, Elizabeth. 1980. *Mother Love: Myth and Reality.* New York: Macmillan.

Barbre, Joy, et al., eds. 1989. *Interpreting Women's Lives: Feminist Theory and Personal Narratives.* Indianapolis: Indiana University Press.

Bassuk, Ellen L. 1986. "Homeless Families: Single Mothers and Their Children in Boston Shelters." In *The Mental Health Needs of Homeless Persons,* ed. Ellen L. Bassuk. San Francisco: Jossey-Bass.

———. 1987. "The Feminization of Homelessness: Homeless Families in Boston Shelters." *American Journal of Social Psychiatry* 7 (1): 19–23.

Berris, David. 1994. "Poverty, Policy, and Performance: The Rhetoric of Poverty in the U.S. Senate." Presented at the ninety-third annual meeting of the American Anthropological Association, November 30–December 4, Atlanta.

Bibliography

Bourgois, Phillipe. 1995. *In Search of Respect: Selling Crack in El Barrio.* Cambridge: Cambridge University Press.

Boxill, Nancy A., ed. 1990. *Homeless Children: The Watchers and the Waiters.* New York: Haworth Press.

Brown, Wendy. 1995. *States of Injury: Power and Freedom in Late Modernity.* Princeton, N.J.: Princeton University Press.

Chodorow, Nancy. 1978. *The Reproduction of Mothering.* Berkeley and Los Angeles: University of California Press.

Collins, Patricia Hill. 1994. "Shifting the Center: Race, Class and Feminist Theorizing about Motherhood." In Glenn et al. 1994.

Connolly, William. 1995. *The Ethos of Pluralization.* Minneapolis: University of Minnesota Press.

Connors, Margaret. 1992. "Risk Perception, Risk Taking and Risk Management among Intravenous Drug Users: Implications for AIDS Prevention." *Social Science Medicine* 34 (6).

———. 1994. "Stories of Pain and the Problem of AIDS Prevention: Injection Drug Withdrawal and Its Effect on Risk Behavior." *Medical Anthropology Quarterly* 8 (4).

Coontz, Stephanie. 1992. *The Way We Never Were: American Families and the Nostalgia Trap.* New York: Basic Books.

Daniels, Cynthia. *At Women's Expense: State, Power and the Politics of Fetal Rights.* Cambridge: Harvard University Press.

Davis, Angela Y. 1983. *Women, Race and Class.* New York: Random House.

Davis, Susan E., ed. 1988. *Women under Attack: Victories, Backlash, and the Fight for Reproductive Freedom.* Committee for Abortion Rights and Against Sterilization Abuse, South End Press pamphlet no. 7.

Dorris, Michael. 1989. *The Broken Cord.* New York: Harper & Row.

Duden, Barbara. 1993. *Disembodying Women: Perspectives on Pregnancy and the Unborn.* Cambridge: Harvard University Press.

Edin, Kathryn, and Laura Lein. 1997. *Making Ends Meet: How Single Mothers Survive Welfare and Low-Wage Work.* New York: Russell Sage Foundation.

Ehrenreich, Barbara, and Frances Fox Piven. 1984. "The Feminization of Poverty." *Dissent* 2 (Spring).

Epstein, William. 1997. *Welfare in America: How Social Science Fails the Poor.* Madison: University of Wisconsin Press.

Eyer, Diane. 1992. *Mother-Infant Bonding: A Science Fiction.* New Haven, Conn.: Yale University Press.

Favret-Saada, Jeanne. 1980. *Deadly Words: Witchcraft in the Bocage.* Cambridge: Cambridge University Press.

Fineman, Martha Albertson, and Isabel Karpin, eds. 1995. *Mothers in Law: Feminist Theory and the Legal Regulation of Motherhood.* New York: Columbia University Press.

Forcey, Linda Rennie. 1994. "Feminist Perspectives on Mothering and Peace." In Glenn et al. 1994.

Foucault, Michel. 1979. *Discipline and Punish: The Birth of the Prison.* New York: Vintage Books.

Frankenberg, Ruth. 1993. *The Social Construction of Whiteness: White Women, Race Matters.* Minneapolis: University of Minnesota Press.

Fraser, Nancy, and Linda Gordon. 1994. "'Dependency' Demystified: Inscriptions of Power in a Keyword of the Welfare State." *Social Politics* (Spring).

Ginsburg, Faye D. 1989. *Contested Lives: The Abortion Controversy in an American Community.* Berkeley and Los Angeles: University of California Press.

Ginsburg, Faye D., and Anna Lowenhaupt Tsing, eds. 1990. *Uncertain Terms: Negotiating Gender in American Culture.* Boston: Beacon Press.

Glenn, Evelyn Nakano, et al., eds. 1994. *Mothering: Ideology, Experience, and Agency.* New York: Routledge Press.

Goffman, Erving. 1963. *Stigma: Notes on the Management of Spoiled Identity.* New York: Simon and Schuster.

Gomez, Laura E. 1997. *Misconceiving Mothers: Legislators, Prosecutors, and the Politics of Prenatal Drug Exposure.* Philadelphia: Temple University Press.

Gordon, Linda. 1994. *Pitied but Not Entitled: Single Mothers and the History of Welfare.* New York: Free Press.

Haraway, Donna. 1991. "Situated Knowledges: The Science Question in Feminism and the Privilege of Partial Perspective." In *Simians, Cyborgs, and Women.* New York: Routledge Press.

Harding, Susan. 1987. "Convicted by the Holy Spirit: The Rhetoric of Fundamental Baptist Conversion." *American Ethnologist* (Fall).

Harris, Kathleen Mullan. 1997. *Teen Mothers and the Revolving Welfare Door.* Philadelphia: Temple University Press.

Hartouni, Valerie. 1991. "Containing Women: Reproductive Discourse in the 1980s." In *Technoculture*, ed. Constance Penley and Andrew Ross. Minneapolis: University of Minnesota Press.

———. 1997. *Cultural Conceptions: On Reproductive Technologies and the Remaking of Life.* Minneapolis: University of Minnesota Press.

Hirsch, Kathleen. 1989. *Songs from the Alley.* New York: Doubleday.

Homes for the Homeless and Columbia University. 1998. *Homeless Families Today: Our Challenge Tomorrow—A Report.* New York: Institute for Children and Poverty. February.

Humphries, Drew. 1999. *Crack Mothers: Pregnancy, Drugs, and the Media.* Athens: Ohio State University Press.

Hymes, Dell, ed. 1972. *Reinventing Anthropology.* New York: Pantheon Books.

Kaplan, Elaine Bell. 1997. *Not Our Kind of Girl: Unraveling the Myths of Black Teenage Motherhood.* Berkeley and Los Angeles: University of California Press.

Katz, Michael B. 1986. *In the Shadow of the Poorhouse: A Social History of Welfare in America.* New York: Basic Books.

Kingfisher, Catherine Pelissier. 1996. *Women in the American Welfare Trap.* Philadelphia: University of Pennsylvania Press.

Ladd-Taylor, Molly, and Lauri Umansky, eds. 1998. *"Bad" Mothers: The Politics of Blame in Twentieth Century America.* New York: New York University Press.

Bibliography

Ladner, Joyce A. 1971. *Tomorrow's Tomorrow: The Black Woman.* New York: Doubleday.

Lambiase, Susan, and James B. Rule. 1996. "Block Grants and the End of Children's Rights." *Dissent* (Fall): 68–73.

Liebow, Elliot. 1993. *Tell Them Who I Am: The Lives of Homeless Women.* New York: Free Press.

Luker, Kristin. 1996. *Dubious Conceptions: The Politics of Teenage Pregnancy.* Cambridge: Harvard University Press.

Martin, Emily. 1987. *The Woman in the Body.* Boston: Beacon Press.

Mink, Gwendolyn. 1995. *The Wages of Motherhood: Inequality in the Welfare State, 1917–1942.* Ithaca, N.Y.: Cornell University Press.

Murphy, Sheigla. 1992. "'It Takes Your Womanhood': Women on Crack." Ph.D. diss., University of California, San Francisco.

Murphy, Sheigla, and Marsha Rosenbaum. 1999. *Pregnant Women on Drugs: Combating Stereotypes and Stigma.* New Brunswick, N.J.: Rutgers University Press.

Nader, Laura. 1972. "Up the Anthropologist—Perspectives Gained from Studying Up." In *Reinventing Anthropology,* ed. Dell Hymes. New York: Pantheon Books.

Newsweek. 1995. "Condemned to Life: After Hearing Disturbing New Details about Susan Smith's Tangled World, a Jury Votes against Death." August 7, 1995, 19.

Nunez, Ralph DaCosta. 1994. *Hopes, Dreams, and Promises: The Future of Homeless Children in America.* New York: Institute for Children and Poverty, Homes for the Homeless.

Paltrow, Lynn. 1992. "Criminal Prosecutions against Pregnant Women: National Update and Overview." Reproductive Freedom Project, American Civil Liberties Union Foundation, April.

Piven, Frances Fox. 1996. "Welfare and the Transformation of Electoral Politics." *Dissent* (Fall): 61–68.

Polakow, Valerie. 1993. *Lives on the Edge: Single Mothers and their Children in the Other America.* Chicago: University of Chicago Press.

Ragoné, Helena. 1994. *Surrogate Motherhood: Conception in the Heart.* Boulder, Colo.: Westview Press.

Reinarman, Craig, and Harry G. Levine. 1997. *Crack in America: Demon Drugs and Social Justice.* Berkeley and Los Angeles: University of California Press.

Rhodes, Lorna Amarsingham. 1990. "Studying Biomedicine as a Cultural System." In *Medical Anthropology: Contemporary Theory and Method,* ed. Thomas M. Johnson and Carolyn F. Sargent. New York: Praeger.

Roberts, Dorothy E. 1991. "Punishing Drug Addicts Who Have Babies: Women of Color, Equality, and the Right to Privacy." *Harvard Law Review* 104 (7).

———. 1995. "Racism and Patriarchy in the Meaning of Motherhood." In Fineman and Karpin 1995.

———. 1996. "The Value of Black Mothers' Work." *Radical America* 26 (1).

Ruddick, Sara. 1989. *Maternal Thinking: Towards a Politics of Peace.* Boston: Beacon Press.

Ryan, Charlotte. 1996. "Battered in the Media: Mainstream News Coverage of Welfare Reform." *Radical America* 26 (9).

Schein, Virginia E. 1995. *Working from the Margins: Voices of Mothers in Poverty.* Ithaca, N.Y.: Cornell University Press.

Scheper-Hughes, Nancy. 1992. *Death without Weeping: The Violence of Everyday Life in Brazil.* Berkeley and Los Angeles: University of California Press.

Skocpol, Theda. 1992. *Protecting Soldiers and Mothers: The Political Origins of Social Policy in the United States.* Cambridge: Harvard University Press.

Skoll, Geoffrey R. 1992. *Walk the Walk and Talk the Talk: An Ethnography of a Drug Abuse Treatment Facility.* Philadelphia: Temple University Press.

Solinger, Rickie. 1992. *Wake up Little Susie: Single Pregnancy and Race before Roe v. Wade.* New York: Routledge.

———. 1994. "Race and 'Value': Black and White Illegitimate Babies, 1945–1965." In Glenn et al. 1994.

———. 1998. "Poisonous Choice." In Ladd-Taylor and Umansky 1998.

Stack, Carol B. 1974. *All Our Kin: Strategies for Survival in a Black Community.* New York: Harper & Row.

Sterk, Claire E. 1999. *Fast Lives: Women Who Use Crack Cocaine.* Philadelphia: Temple University Press.

Todorov, Tzvetan. 1985. *The Conquest of America: The Question of the Other,* trans. Richard Howard. New York: Harper & Row.

Toth, Jennifer. 1997. *Orphans of the Living: Stories of America's Children in Foster Care.* New York: Simon and Schuster.

Tsing, Anna Lowenhaupt. 1990. "Monster Stories: Women Charged with Perinatal Endangerment." In *Uncertain Terms: Negotiating Gender in American Culture,* ed. Faye Ginsburg and Anna Lowenhaupt Tsing. Boston: Beacon Press.

———. 1993. *In the Realm of the Diamond Queen.* Princeton, N.J.: Princeton University Press.

Waldorf, Dan, Craig Reinarman, and Sheigla Murphy. 1992. *Cocaine Changes.* Philadelphia: Temple University Press.

White, Lucie E. 1996. "On the 'Consensus' to End Welfare: Where Are the Women's Voices?" *Radical America* 26 (9).

Wray, Matt, and Annalee Newitz. 1997. *White Trash: Race and Class in America.* New York: Routledge.

Index

Deborah R. Connolly received her Ph.D. in anthropology from the University of California, Santa Cruz. She is a researcher at Edgewood Center for Children and Families in San Francisco.